SMALL BUSINESS: THE INDEPEN

MACMILLAN SMALL BUSINESS SERIES
Series Editors: Jim Dewhurst and Paul Burns

The books in this series present their subject-matter comprehensively and in a sophisticated manner with more conceptual underpinning than has previously been provided.

The series is intended primarily for undergraduate and postgraduate students taking small business and related courses at universities and polytechnics. Books in the series will also be suitable for those working for professional examinations and for well-informed managers of small and growing businesses.

PUBLISHED

Paul Burns and Jim Dewhurst (eds), *Small Business and Entrepreneurship*
Paul Burns and Jim Dewhurst (eds), *Small Business in Europe*
Gary Davies and Kim Harris, *Small Business: The Independent Retailer*
Jim Dewhurst and Paul Burns, *Small Business: Planning, Finance and Control*
Terry Hill, *Small Business: Production/Operations Management*
Derek Waterworth, *Small Business: Marketing for the Small Business*

SMALL BUSINESS

The Independent Retailer

Gary Davies and Kim Harris

M
MACMILLAN

First published 1990

Published by
MACMILLAN EDUCATION LTD
Houndmills, Basingstoke, Hampshire RG21 2XS
and London
Companies and representatives
throughout the world

Printed in Hong Kong

British Library Cataloguing in Publication Data
Davies, Gary
Small business.
1. Great Britain. Retailing
I. Title II. Harris, Kim
658.8′7′00941
ISBN 0–333–48836–9 (hardcover)
ISBN 0–333–48837–7 (paperback)

Contents

List of Tables

List of Figures

Foreword

Both Napoleon and Adam Smith have been credited with coining the label of a nation of shopkeepers for the British. The image such a description conjurs up is of a substantial proportion of the population donning striped aprons or dark suits each morning and rolling up the shutters on the front of a business that is their own. While retailing accounts for almost as large a proportion of the work-force today as it ever did, today's retail scene is not one dominated by the independent owner. A steady decline in the share of trade through the smaller enterprise could be extrapolated to the point where the multiple retailers account for almost all retail sales. But such an approach ignores the reality that the smaller business still accounts for over a third of turnover in an economic sector that is displaying above average growth. It ignores the reality that few multiple chains suddenly appear without first having been a single enterprise. Such is the dynamic, fast-changing and competitive nature of retailing that the the future of retailing lies substantially in the hands of some businesses that are today no more than a good idea, flourishing in a small corner of the land. With ambition and some luck there will be the next generation of Body Shop, Tie Rack and Sock Shop, the new Laura Ashley and a Benetton or two. Michael Marks began in Leeds over a hundred years ago with a single market stall: such success is still possible today.

However, many small retailers have no such ambitions and seek only the objectives of profitable survival and the independence of owning and operating their own business. This book addresses both types of independent retail business, and examines small-scale retailing from the perspective of those who seek to grow and those who seek mainly to enhance what will be unlikely to become a multiple retail business.

Both share common problems. The competitive environment is changing. From an era of being able to compete by offering a broad range of products and having a local presence, to one where a more precise business direction is essential. The 1980s saw the emergence and growth of niche retailing. The lessons of the success of niche retailing need to be learned and understood.

After placing the independent retail business into context, the book seeks to identify how best such organisations can compete. Later chapters deal with topics introduced earlier in greater depth. The book ends with a number of real-life case studies, selected to illustrate the authors' views and ideas, but also to allow the reader to come to his or her own conclusions on the best way forward for the independent retailer.

GARY DAVIES
KIM HARRIS

CHAPTER 1

The Independent Retailer

Setting the scene

Described recently as a 'paradigm of the enterprise culture'[1] retailing would appear to look poised for a prosperous future. 1988 was expected to herald the largest year-on-year increase in retail sales since 1980, jumping 9½ per cent to £103 billion.[2] Employment in retailing in relation to other sectors of the economy also looked healthy, showing growth since 1978 of 6.9 per cent, compared to manufacturing industry's decline of 25.9 per cent. Faced with up-market facilities, competitive prices and a wider choice of quality goods, customers appeared to remain only too eager to line the retailers' pockets with money. Although precise estimations of consumer spending obviously depend on underlying general economic growth and budget decisions, predictions for spending up to 1990 and beyond looked encouraging with average increases expected year-on-year in real terms over 3 per cent. The improved public profile of many leading retailers for example, Anita Roddick, George Davies, Terrance Conran and Sophie Mirman have improved retail share performances and stimulated interest and more crucially investment from home and abroad. The trend looks set to continue as the work of creating a united Europe by 1992 through the relaxation of financial, legal and fiscal barriers to trade gains momentum.

An optimistic overview. But will the potential benefits be experienced evenly by all retailers irrespective of mode of operation, number of employees, location, range of products offered and prices charged? The answer is obviously no. As the title of the book implies, the authors wish to focus on the smaller retailer to try to locate their position within the sector as a whole. In chapter 2 a strengths, weaknesses, opportunities and threats analysis is undertaken in an attempt to make the overall picture clearer. The position of the large retail outlets (Asda, MFI, and so on) has been widely commented on in retail literature, but the 'cinderella' sector of the retail business community has to a large extent been neglected.[3] The authors hope to have remedied this situation by the end of the book.

The chapter will continue with a consideration of a number of definitional problems. First, what the authors feel can be included in a definition of retailing and secondly, what can be classified as a small retailer. Clarification of these issues will set the scene for the remainder of the book. The role and importance of the smaller retailer in relation to retailing past and present is then discussed. The chapter ends with a brief overview of the various forms of government assistance available to small retailers and a number of comments made about the increasing importance of the 'European' dimension.

Definitional problems

The scope of retailing

A dictionary definition of retailing is normally in terms such as 'the sale of goods individually or in small quantities to consumers'. Such a simple definition has serious flaws when trying to find a definition appropriate to retailing today. A quick visual comparison between a high street in somewhere like Macclesfield in the North of England today and the same area 20 years ago would reinforce the idea that definitions of retailing appropriate in the past do not reflect the real nature of retail businesses today. Estate agents and travel agencies feature more prominently as do specialist retail outlets aiming their products at a narrowly-defined target audience, for example, Butterfly, the colourful sweet shop. The indices of consumer spending reflect the changing priorities of retail customers with leisure activities, finance and housing playing a far more important role. According to statistics on economic trends, major growth areas for spending are presently (and will continue to be for the foreseeable future) DIY products, spending on motor vehicles, petrol and accessories, air travel, telecommunications and video hire. Retailers have had to alter the nature of their businesses to mirror these changes.

Many pieces of legislation established 30 or 40 years ago to regulate retail activities are also inappropriate to the retailing environment of the 1980s, the most obvious being the 1950 Shops Act which guides shop opening hours. Much of the pressure for reform of the 1950s Shops Act stemmed from the fact that the list of exempt items which *could* be sold in shops on a Sunday (outlined in Schedule V of the Act) were widely inappropriate to purchasing priorities of consumers in the 1980s. Schedule V allows shops to sell 'newly-cooked provisions and cooked or partly cooked tripe, as well as tobacco and smokers' requisites'. Both may have been important in 1950 due to the lack of cold storage facilities in the average household and the importance of tobacco, but are no longer relevant to the affluent, health-conscious society of today.

Just as the law needs updating from time to time, so too, in the authors' view, do current definitions of retailing. The Department of Trade and Industry, Business Statistics Office, classify retailing in their Business Monitor by Kind of Business (KOB). In most cases the KOB classification of a business is divided on the basis of the main commodity sold, that is, the KOB is *product* based. Recent research has criticised the classification system for not being able to accommodate the consumer-orientated retailer like Next, for example, who market a 'lifestyle' throughout their product range.[4]

The general conclusion is that retail definitions do not take a 'broad' enough view of the sector.

In order to obtain the scope of coverage required in this book, the authors have chosen the following definition of *retailing*:

'Retailing is the provision (or the process of providing) for mutual benefit goods and services to ultimate consumers or those buying on behalf of ultimate consumers.'[5]

The definition will stand as justification for use of the retail examples cited throughout the book.

With the continued growth of 'niche' retailers specialising in distinct product areas there would be a danger that they would not fall within the more conventional definitions of retailing and therefore escape comment. In the authors' view the definition chosen allows the necessary scope for a review of retailing today. The definition was tested at Manchester Polytechnic recently in relation to a mature applicant applying for the Retail Marketing Degree Course there. One of the selection criteria was that he should have a substantial amount of retail-related experience. Abiding by the definition the interviewers were obliged to consider his five years' experience with a major High Street bank as equivalent to others who gained their experience with multiple grocery retailers.

As the reader will see in chapter 5, principles of retail layout and design can just as readily be applied to banks, building societies and insurance agencies as small grocery outlets.

The question of size

Analysis of existing definitions

The second definitional issue which needs to be clarified is what exactly do we mean by 'small' retailers. Numerous ideas have been put forward in an attempt to produce a coherent classification for 'small'. The 1986 Companies Act adopted three separate criteria to define small businesses generally based on turnover, capital and number of employees. A retail business would be classed as 'small' if it met any two of the following three conditions: fewer than 50 employees, sales of up to £2m and balance sheet asset value of less than £175 000. Most statistical sources on retailing use shop numbers to define various subgroups. The Retail Inquiry statistics refer to single outlet retailers, small multiple retailers (having two to nine outlets) and large multiple retailers with ten or more. The Bolton Report back in 1971 rejected the statistical approach in favour of a definition which attempted to account for the 'human aspects of the small business'. For a retail business to be classed as small it was important to prove that it had a relatively small share of the market, was managed by its owners or part-owners in a personalised way and not through the medium of a formalised management structure. Finally it had to be independent in the sense that it did not form part of a larger enterprise and that the owner managers should be free from outside control in taking their principal decisions.[6]

Another definition from the point of view of employment law classifies a small firm as one with four or less employees (for health and safety legislation) or 20 or less (for unfair dismissal cases).[7]

Many commentators rely on the government data on VAT-registered businesses to operate their definitions.[8] However, with the VAT threshold for registration set at £22 100 (1988 figures) such classifications could be criticised for excluding many very small retail operators, who may not have registered, as well as failing to take into account the high percentage which may be registered at some point but fail to continue trading after the first few years. Although the 1986 Inquiry Statistics have made allowances for businesses registered below the mandatory threshold for VAT registrations, it still excludes a proportion of the small retail sector.

While there may be relative merits in each definition, the authors' view is that none is sufficient for the purposes of discussing the performance of small retailers. The major problem is one of comparability of types of small retail operations. Product and services differences mean that realistic comparisons between retailers based on criteria like number of employees, turnover, and so on, could only be drawn if comments were very sector specific, for example, small grocery outlets stocking certain ranges of merchandise, small florists, small petrol stations, and so on. As *Skidmore*[9] demonstrated, current government KOB classifications for *types* of retailers are not taxonomically sound, and it will be some time before *size* distinctions can be made within sectors. This general criticism can be applied to all definitions, but some specific ideas need to be discussed. For example, if the reader accepted the Bolton Committee definition that small retail businesses would not have to be part of a larger enterprise how would one class franchised retailers? One of the arguments to be developed in this book is that convenience store franchising has developed as a means by which small retailers can order their business and survive in the competitive retail environment. Few franchisees the authors have met would agree that simply because they may have invested their capital in the operation, they are no longer small or independent, free from outside control in taking their principal decisions.[10]

Different business objectives

Another problem with placing too tight a reign on any definition of what is small relates to the concept of time or stage of development a business is at. A common assumption made by writers on small enterprises is that their owners are all constantly striving to make their business bigger, leading ultimately to market domination.

Although there are many examples in retailing today of companies which began as very small operators but have expanded to dominate a particular market sector, there are just as many examples of businesses which have deliberately chosen to remain small and serve the same market as they did when they originally set up. At what stage in the development of a business can it no longer be classed as small? Kwik Fit, for example, began in 1971 as one tyre and accessory supply shop in an Edinburgh backstreet. Seventeen years later they had mushroomed to become one of the largest independent parts and replacement groups in Europe. In contrast, Mr Bhati, in Case Study A, had no desire to achieve expansion in the grocery market as long as he could generate sufficient income from his business to support his family. The same retailing principles and techniques can be applied to the business irrespective of the owner's future plans and aspirations for the business.

A flexible approach

Due to the broad applicability and tolerance to retailers generally of many of the concepts discussed in the book, the authors have decided to a large extent to allow the reader's own perception of small to guide them through the text. Justification for this approach comes not only from rejection of definitions currently available, but, more importantly, from speaking to retailers themselves. Michael Dunn of the Happy Nut House (Case Study B) was responsible for the third largest health food chain in Britain but still considered his business as small. In contrast, Mr Bhati, a grocer with a net profit of about £300 per week and one shop in Richmond, perhaps understandably considered himself as small. Despite this flexible approach the idea that small is a relative concept is still important. Small retailers should be compared to large operators who clearly have the ability to exploit scale economies through bulk purchasing and ultimately lower consumer prices, and also the financial resources to enable them to employ specialist management in-house, for example, marketing managers and accountants. Major multiples like Tesco, Asda and Sainsburys would meet this criteria.

Although the authors have chosen to remain flexible in their definition of small it is hoped that the examples used throughout the book will help the reader to develop their own perception to what the notion of a smaller retailer refers.

Despite the authors' implied criticisms of existing classifications of small retailers, a number of them have been used in the next section of this chapter to provide statistical data to demonstrate how the role and importance of the smaller retailer has changed over time.

The role and importance of the smaller retailer

The most noticeable threat to the small businesses' position in the retail environment has undoubtedly come from the rise in power of the major multiple operators.

Kirby and Dawson feel this increase in power has been made possible with the introduction of the concepts of self-service and supermarkets, 'radical or revolutionary' changes in the retail area.[11] They identify other changes which have had an impact on the small retailer such as consumer demand for new products and the increase in personal mobility, but stress that these should only be regarded as 'evolutionary' development.

Whatever the historic justification for the change, the market share of the multiples has been increasing at the expense of the share of the independents and co-ops (Figure 1.1 illustrates this point).

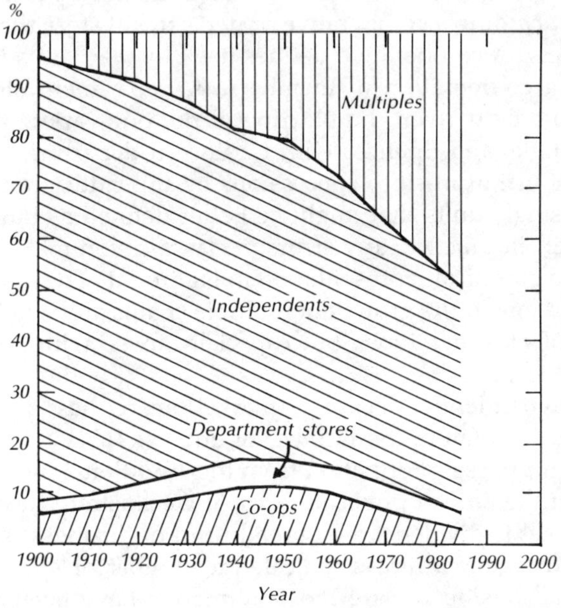

Figure 1.1 Share of total retail sales

Sources: A number of sources have been used to construct Figure 1.1. The major source prior to the 1950s is Jeffreys.[12] Thereafter government statistics from the Census of Distribution and the more recent Retail Enquiry have been used. Estimates by the authors have been used to blend the two main data sources, the major problem being the fact that some department stores could be classified as independents, others as multiples and some belong to, or are, co-operatives.

Table 1.1 Changes in shop numbers

Classification	*No. of shops 1984*	*Percentage of sales 1984*	*% change in shop nos 1976–84*
Single outlet retailers	201 633	29.5	−12.8
Independents with 2–9 shops	73 670	12.8	− 6.4
Co-ops	5 813	5.3	−47.7
Multiples	62 037	52.4	−23.1
TOTAL	343 153	100.0	−12.1[a]

Note:
a average.
Source: Derived from Retail Inquiry 1976, 1980, 1984.

The authors have used the convention of defining a multiple as any business excluding a co-operative or department store that has ten or more outlets. A co-operative defines itself by way of its legal constitution as a co-operation of members. A department store is most difficult to define given the blurring of the one variety chain stores such as Marks and Spencer with traditional department stores, the substantial use of in-store concessions by the latter group, and that some are single units that might be better defined as independents.

However, in practice, any errors in classification make little difference to the graphical representation in Figure 1.1. The main trends of a sustained one in the growth of multiple chains and a fall in share of business of all other types but especially those with less than ten outlets are clear.

The independent's declining market share has also been accompanied by a fall in the number of outlets (Table 1.1).

Although precise information from the 1986 Retail Inquiry was not available at the time of publication Table 1.2 illustrates how the share of the market is divided up by broad Kind of Business (KOB).

Within the general areas indicated a number of specific areas in which small businesses are most numerous have been performing particularly well since 1980. Off-licences increased their share of all retail sales by 11 per cent between 1980 and 1985, compared with a decline for grocers of 17 per cent. Jewellers, booksellers and stationers have also performed well with increases in share of 12 per cent and 9 per cent respectively.

Apart from the last few comments, however, a statistical overview of the independent retailers' position would hardly give much cause for optimism.

Table 1.2 Share of retail sales by kind of business

Business	1984 No. of business	1984 No. of outlets	1984 Turnover	1986 No. of business	1986 No. of outlets	1986 Turnover	% change in turnover
Food retailers	81 680	105 953	30 885	77 301	100 171	34 761	+13
Drink, confectionary, tobacco (includes off licences)	43 226	56 499	8 461	44 379	56 858	9 969	+18
Clothing, footwear, leather goods retailers	32 000	58 552	7 641	32 711	58 874	9 198	+24
Household goods (includes electrical, DIY)	42 916	60 104	12 105	42 785	60 839	14 718	+22
Other non-food retailers (includes jewellers, newsagents)	38 617	50 858	6 749	39 395	51 357	8 234	+18
Mixed retail businesses	5 644	11 231	15 639	4 853	10 077	18 224	+17
Hire and repair businesses	2 848	6 531	1 114	2 861	5 783	1 319	+18

Note: Within sectors, largest increases for electrical/DIY, off-licences, jewellers and newsagents

Niche retailing

A more flexible and appropriate use of the definition of 'small' undoubtedly strengthens the smaller retailers' position in the eyes of critics. According to a recent review of the retail sector 'Bigger isn't always better', Sainsburys and M & S should take a few tips from Tie Rack and Sock Shop.[13] The report goes on to say that the difficulties currently experienced by the likes or Asda, MFI and other larger outlets (or Goliaths as they are referred to in the report) have forced them to adopt forms of 'niche' retailing attempting to corner a specific market segment. One of the most obvious examples of this could be found at the Bradford Asda store where a Body Centre specialising in health care products was set up by the company and located away from the main body of the store in the shopping mall in the entrance. Specialist staff had been recruited from outside the organisation to manage and control the 'shop within a shop' arrangement. This is just one example of how a concept which originated in the small retail sector has been used by a large operator to differentiate itself from the rest of the market-place.

The growth of convenience retailing

The idea that the smaller retailer has a role to play in complimenting the activities of the very large stores has been expressed by other writers. Because of the specialist nature of many of the products supplied by small retailers, for example, grocery top-ups and emergencies, the small shop fulfils an important secondary role within the distributive system, complementing rather than competing with big business.[14]

Convenience stores, following the experiences in the USA, can be cited as a good example, emerging to satisfy a need for *local* shops. Although there appears to be some conflict over precisely what can be defined as a convenience store, one definition refers to:

> a self-service store between 1000 and 3000 sq. ft located close to housing with some parking facilities, offering a wide range of goods including grocery products, chemists, sundries, alcohol and possibly other lines including video hire, fast foods or petrol with opening hours including Sundays.[15]

This 'relatively' new convenience store sector is said to be expanding at the same rate as the UK fast-food outlets some seven years ago. It is a trend that can be observed in other parts of the world. The convenience store chain 7-Eleven, for example, has outlets in Australia, Sweden, Britain and Japan.

The convenience trading platform is undoubtedly strengthening the position of many smaller retailers.

Specialist goods and services

The emergence of specialist small retailers basing their product offer on a carefully selected target audience emphasises their capacity to provide the variety consumers are demanding in today's market-place. Carefully planned design techniques incorporated into both product and store presentation have helped to create sufficient consumer interest in smaller outlets to attract them away from traditional high street stores. Specialist product offers are also being improved with the incorporation of various ethnic groups into the small retail sector. The increasing involvement of Asian retailers is perhaps the most obvious to the casual observer. Some writers have estimated that almost one-third of all small grocers are now Asian. Although the authors' own research indicates that the lack of business management skills is prohibiting the short-term growth in this group, their presence in the retail market-place is helping to educate consumers to appreciate new tastes and life-styles. Patterns of consumer spending reflect adventurous changes in attitudes towards foreign goods and service. Although many of the larger retailers already recognise the growth potential of this particular market segment (the foreign goods market), they appear to lack both the flexibility in the short term and a genuine desire to accept such products into their portfolio. Although Asian and Chinese ethnic products, for example, are featured in stores in areas with a high percentage of Asians and Chinese in their catchment area, marketing managers and buyers appear reluctant to consider the possibility that a similar demand could be generated from an indigenous white population.

Forms of assistance available to small retailers

One factor which illustrates the importance of the smaller operator in retailing is the amount of interest governments appear to be taking in their position. Along with other small business enterprises there have been numerous policy initiatives taken over the past ten years designed to promote small businesses and self-employment in particular. These initiatives have normally been backed by various resources whether direct finance or manpower subsidies. Leaflets are continually being produced by the Department of Trade and Industry giving information to small businesses about assistance available. Retailers are obviously included although strict 'size' definitions are enforced to prevent abuse of the system. The particular stage of development that a retailer is at is also relevant when applying for assistance, that is, whether start-up or development. The next section reviews a number of the more important sources of help available to the small retailer.

Financial assistance

In 1981 the government introduced a *small firms loan guarantee scheme* to help the smaller operator to raise capital. With a variable rate of interest, financial assistance was available on loans of up to £75 000 for between 2 and 7 years. Seventy per cent of the loan was guaranteed to the borrower by the Department of the Environment in exchange for which the business paid a premium of 2.5 per cent to the Department on that guaranteed portion. The scheme was criticised for being too expensive when other forms of assistance were available more cheaply. Elsewhere others have spoken highly of the initiatives stating that many businesses would not have got off the ground without such assistance.[16] Indeed, Sock Shop was launched with £45 000 of loans under the scheme, after banks refused to lend money to its founders without such security.

The Business Expansion Scheme was another financial scheme aimed at helping the smaller retailer to attract capital. It allowed outside investors to buy ordinary shares in any qualifying business up to a maximum of £40 000 and obtain tax relief on their investment. Again, although the scheme was criticised for serving the interests of the investor rather than small businesses themselves,[17] it was praised as being a source of finance on a relatively small scale for both new and established businesses. (The Department of Employment's Small Firms Service as well as small firms units of the major banks provide current details of these and other sources of financial assistance available to retailers.)

Other forms of assistance in 1989

Although financial assistance is often crucial to the initial success or failure of small retail operations, once established, there are numerous agencies and schemes available which will help the business develop.

The Rural Development Commission's government-funded body runs a business service with offices situated in every rural county of England. The Commission was formed in 1988 by merging COSIRA (the Council for Small Industries in Rural Areas) with the Development Commission. By offering practical assistance to small retailers in isolated locations the Commission helps to run a business within the rural communities. They provide technical and professional advice in all aspects of retailing, and frequently hold business seminars at reduced rates for owners. Again, definitions of shop size and stage of development are taken into account when offering assistance to retailers.

The Training Agency, previously the Manpower Services Commission, funds a large number of training courses which may be relevant to retailers. Although these tend to be aimed mainly at businesses, many focus on developing managerial skills (particularly financial skills) which can be beneficial to established retailers. As the strengths and weaknesses analysis in chapter 2 indicates, smaller retailers are often unable to maximise growth potential due to a lack of business acumen. Research indicates that most of the problem stems from the fact that retailers are unaware of training assistance available to themselves or their employees whether free or at subsidised rates.

Voluntary associations

Apart from the government-sponsored bodies mentioned above, there are numerous self-financed organisations which have been set up specifically to help retail businesses. Although some will be referred to directly throughout the book, a full list of addresses is included at the end of the final chapter (see before Case Studies). The British Independent Grocers Association and the National Association of Shopkeepers are just two which are aimed directly at smaller retailers. The British Franchise Association also provides information and guidance for retailers considering this type of business operation.

Voluntary associations fall into two categories, those offering a source of advice, expertise and a forum, and those that facilitate the 'independent retailers' business. The latter extend to full-blown franchises, but include voluntary chains such as Spar which offer group purchasing and a trading format as well as many of the advantages of the first category. Interflora is another slightly different example where the members agree some common trading formats but where the association is more concerned with operating a specific service that is an adjunct to the main business of most members.

The European dimension

In the present economic climate a discussion of assistance available to small retailers would not be complete without some mention of the encouragement presently being given to small businesses prepared to operate in the European market. Within Europe as a whole retailing is the second most important economic activity. Although the BOTB (British Overseas Trade Board) has been in existence for some time with regional offices offering practical and financial help to retailers looking to expand into European markets, the focus of attention most recently has become Europe. The institutions of European government (including the Commission, the Council, the European Court of Justice and the European Parliament), in conjunction with national governments, have been busy passing directives to be enforced in member countries aimed at creating a fully-integrated European market by 1992. Although the precise impact of the removal of fiscal, technical and legal barriers to trade on the retail sector have yet to be clarified in detail, there are certain issues which will undoubtedly have an impact on the smaller operator (see Appendix to this chapter). To ensure that small businesses are given enough information to be able to respond, the European Commission set up a task force for SME units (small medium enterprise units) in each of the European countries in 1988 with a number of centres which convey information directly from Brussels to the SME. At the time of writing there were four such Infocentres in Britain linking into existing organisations giving advice to small businesses. The Infocentre in London is located with one of the London small firms offices[18] and staff are available to answer any questions small retailers may have about the opportunities 1992 may offer.

The objective of this chapter has been to 'set the scene' for the rest of the book. A number of definitional problems have been clarified and the relative position and importance of the small retailer in both the UK and Europe has been considered.

A more detailed analysis of the small retailers' position is given in chapter 2. The remaining chapters concentrate on specific areas of retailing offering useful ideas about how practitioners can apply retail theory in practice. The case studies at the end of the book illustrate real examples of retailers who either have benefited, or perhaps could benefit, from the ideas put forward.

Keypoint summary

- Problems in researching small retail businesses stem from lack of uniformity in defining both the scope of retailing itself and classifications of size. The authors prefer a flexible definition based on retailer perceptions and experience.

- Statistics show a decline in market share of independents and fall in number of outlets. Certain sectors of retailing however, dominated by smaller operations, show impressive market-share increases.
- The independent retailer has been prominent in the development of 'niche' retailing offering specialist goods and services as well as in convenience trading.
- Assistance is available both at home and abroad for small retailers although its existence is rarely publicised sufficiently.

Appendix to Chapter 1

1992 – Some changes of interest to retailers

Directives from Brussels	*Potential impact*
Harmonisation of indirect taxes: EEC proposal 2 rates of VAT.4–9%, for basic socially-important goods, such as food, books, transport. 15–20% for other goods and services	• VAT on food, children's clothing, books, newspapers • Impact on consumer spending: alcohol +25%, books & newspaper −5%, children's clothing −10%, cigarettes +3%, food −1%, petrol −4%
Directives relating to technological innovations	• Increase in teleshopping, video catalogues, electronic payment systems (direct selling by screen currently done by 40 operators in US and operations underway in Canada, Japan, Italy, France)
Directives concerning other operational issues	• Creation of the single person company • Promotion of franchising as a mode of operation • Product restrictions in door-to-door sales operations • Uniform trading hours widespread, Sunday trading • Increase in merger activity and creation of European brands

CHAPTER 2

Strengths and Weaknesses of the Smaller Retailer

In true marketing fashion the next stage in the study of the 'small' retailer arena must be a strengths, weaknesses, opportunities and threats (SWOT) analysis of the sector. The authors' optimism for the future of the smaller shopkeeper already evident from chapter 1 indicates that the strengths and opportunities analysis will act as a starting point for discussion.

Strengths and opportunities

Customer contact

Students and practitioners of business are constantly told that long-term success depends on the ability of the organisation whether large or small to respond to the 'needs' and desires of customers. The fact that the small retailer has greater contact with the customers it serves provides the first major source of strength that needs to be capitalised on. For example, one small grocer recently demonstrated the importance of responding to customers' comments and benefited to the tune of an additional £800 per week – a net increase of 12 per cent on his existing turnover. Although already dabbling in a small selection of fresh meats in his store, his customers suggested that he employed a butcher and widened his product range. Within two months he had set up a preparation room, equipped the area with a chopping block, knives, cleavers and scales, and employed a part-time butcher to serve behind the extended delicatessen counter.[1]

Although this may seem like an obvious adjustment, a large multiple retailer with 350 outlets and a uniform image to maintain in each would have difficulty in implementing this change even if customers demanded it in every area. The important point is that the impetus for change came from the customers.

The symbol group SPAR, realising the value of customer suggestions, have placed 'suggestion boxes' into each of their 2550 units calling on shoppers to tell them exactly what they want to see in store.

Although the average amount spent in smaller outlets in the grocery trade is relatively small (estimates of £3 average sale per visit versus £40 for a multiple are common), the stores benefit from frequency of customer visits. The same customer is likely to visit the store once a day rather than once a week due to the nature of the purchase.

Social function

In a relaxed atmosphere customers are only too willing to air their views. Many writers have commented on the importance of the small retailer in fulfilling a 'social' need within the community it serves. Customers often go to the shop for a chance to 'gossip', whether the conversation revolves around the products, or the weather, or the latest television programme. The fact that every customer visits more often means that they get to know one another and shopping becomes part of a wider social experience. Kirby comments that the local shop in both urban and rural settings is frequently a focus of community life and point of contact, with the shopkeeper acting as 'transmitter of information, confident and social therapist'.[2]

One of the authors' own experiences within a large retail organisation has led to the opinion that the importance of the sales assistant as a means of obtaining the information from customers is often undervalued. Everyone is aware that direct communication channels are the most effective and allow little room for distortion. Although sales assistants are the people in immediate contact with the customers, little time is given to train them to interpret effectively the feedback they receive from shoppers. A smaller retailer can respond to his customers' needs more accurately as well as more quickly.

Inherent flexibility

The ability to respond quickly to customer requests could be incorporated simply into the strength of *flexibility*. Independents like the Lalani Group, which has grown from a corner shop to a £65m turnover group that includes Europa stores and I. Eveshed and Sons, see this flexibility as a key strength in their operation. Although they have invested in establishing a uniform 'convenience' image throughout their stores, they feel that they have maintained a high level of flexibility to 'bend and change' their outlets to suit the locality. For example, if there is no off-licence in the area, the company will start one accordingly; if there is a gap for a confectionery, tobacco and newsagent type of service, emphasis will go on that, whilst still providing the rest of the services. Large multiples who are highly centralised often lack total flexibility. For example, customer and market-trend data might indicate that an Asian or Chinese shop within a shop operation could prove to be profitable in four stores but they would not have the flexibility to co-ordinate product buying and merchandising procedures for such a small-scale operation. A small retailer could remerchandise a section in the store within a matter of days.

Diversity of operation

Flexibility has allowed the small retail sector to develop another strength to help combat the competition and polarisation in retailing today, diversity in mode of operation. The emergence of less conventional forms of small retail enterprise has been the major reason for the necessity for the 'broad' definition of retailing outlined in chapter 1. Probably the most obvious of these from a retail point of view is the development of franchising as a type of operation. This will be discussed in more detail in the final chapter of the book. Briefly, it consists of a host organisation (franchisor) which has developed a product or service and established contractual relationships with franchises who operate under the franchisor trade name according to a format specified by the franchisor. The franchised enterprises are legally independent of the franchisor.

Although franchising generally has been long established in some areas as a method of small business operation (brewer-tenanted public houses, car distribution), one of the largest areas of expansion has been in retail food franchising. Small shops in a wide range of retail sectors, from off-licences to chemists under threat from the multiples, have been only too willing to respond to this new form of business arrangement. Small stores have adopted the uniform facia of a chain name such as Sperrings, or Circle 'K', and injected specified amounts of capital in return for help in administrating, marketing and controlling the business. Many of the food retailer franchises have adopted the 'convenience' trading pattern which originated in the USA and is proving to be a major strength in the development of the small retail sector. Recent estimates from *Retail Business*[3] put the turnover of the convenience sector at around £1bn per year, increasing at a rate of 25–30 per cent annually. Small retailers are increasingly showing a willingness to vary their product mix in response to the success of the new trading pattern. A successful trading format for a convenience store nowadays is one which combines the grocer, confectioner, tobacconist and newsagent (CTN), off-licence, baker, milkman, chemist, greengrocer and take-away, and suits the needs of the community. No longer does it appear to be sufficient to remain simply as a CTN. The advertisement in Figure 2.1 details one franchising package offered to retailers.

Franchised stores are not confined solely to food retailing. Perhaps one of the most obvious examples of a franchised clothing operation is the Tie Rack Trading Ltd, who operate 105 franchised branches in strategic locations throughout the UK. Others include the Body and Face Place, franchised retailers of back-to-nature Edinburgh Aromatics products, and Apollo window blinds franchises. For an investment of around £63 000 in 1988, 70 per cent of which can be financed through the major clearing banks, Apollo franchisees receive a comprehensive package including all the elements necessary to establish a successful retail/manufacturing business.[4]

Figure 2.1 Advertisement for prospective franchises

Control

The different forms of retail trading operation which have been emerging in the 1980s have led to an increasingly diverse and differentiated network of shops. Combined with the amalgamation of retailers into what can be described as Mega retailers (Storehouse, The Dee Corporation) these changes have posed problems for large retailers in terms of control. Heavy investment in new technology has been occurring in an attempt to streamline distribution operations and point-of-sale transactions as well as cut down on the major problem of shrinkage. (Marks and Spencer are reported to lose £1 million per week in stock and other losses.) It is in the area of control that the efficient small retailer has a potential advantage.

A simple but efficiently-operated stock control system allows the smaller traders' capital (which is not then tied up in dead stock) to be invested in new products/store layout, and so on, as well as providing up-to-date knowledge relating to fast-selling products. Computer information systems are generally introduced to provide faster response times for decision-making by larger companies. An efficient small retailer with a simple and effective system can implement a decision change immediately. A larger retailer may be aware of the problems but still has immediate implementation difficulties.

Tight business control also relates to the retailer's labour force, the largest cost under direct control of retailers. Detailed analysis of busy and slack trading patterns allows the small retailer to staff the store more appropriately to the business needs. Close supervision of employees also ensures that another major shrinkage area, employee theft, is kept at a minimum. More staff increases the potential for dishonest workers to slip through the large-retailer safety net. It must be noted at this point that the preceding paragraphs emphasise a 'potential strength' for the smaller retailer that will only be capitalised on if control procedures are implemented efficiently.

Entry and exit barriers

The strengths of the smaller retailer are more numerous in reality than illustrated so far in this chapter. Others will become more obvious as the reader explores the rest of the book. Another strength that is also a potential weakness includes the lack of barriers to entry for people wishing to set up their own retail business (apart from the capital to purchase the outlet) and the existence of government policies designed to encourage small business growth. At the same time the smaller trader can decide quickly to drop a trading format that is in decline and move into another product area without worrying about such things as stock market opinion. The strengths analysis highlights the fact that the efficient small store does fulfil and has the potential to continue to fulfil an important social and economic function in a modern distributive system.

Weaknesses and threats

The weaknesses of the smaller retailer appear to be much more widely documented within current literature. The commentary usually begins with some statistics showing evidence of small business failure followed by detailed analysis of the reasons which caused the demise. Small-scale retailing has often been described as 'one of the easiest ways of losing the savings of a lifetime'. The decline in the number of independent retail shops cannot be denied. Bamfield[5] uses statistics derived from the Retail Inquiry which states that the total number of retail outlets fell by 166 000 or 33 per cent between 1971 and 1984 and that 88 per cent of that decline occurred in the independent sector.

However, many of the reasons identified in the literature to explain the poor performance are not specifically related to the retail sector. For this reason our comments on weakness and threats will be directed towards *small retailer* deficiencies rather than those of small businesses generally.

The multiple threat

Most obvious amongst the weaknesses and threats are those posed by the large retail multiples who assert pressure on the independent to keep customer prices down through exploitation of bulk purchasing power and supplier control. Their rapid rise to power, and their strategies for competing with the independent sector, are discussed in depth in chapter 3. To a large extent this weakness is 'uncontrollable' although, as the following chapter indicates, the smaller retailer can react positively and should not be content to sit back and be beaten.

Lack of professionalism

The second major weakness which is more controllable relates to the attitude and approach to business displayed by a small retailer owner or manager. Studies on manager/owners motivation to their business have indicated that all too often, as a result of a financial windfall, such as a redundancy payment, or as a result of a personal ambition, the owner of a small store has ventured into retailing with insufficient business preparation or acumen. Professionalism is a key factor to the success of both large- and small-scale retailers, and tends to be overlooked because of the ease of entry into small-scale retailing. Although owner managers often display characteristics such as motivation, hard work and flexibility, they appear to have little financial awareness as to how profits are made or costs incurred.

Recent research into ethnic retail operations by one of the authors emphasises the difficulty faced by Asian retailers in this area. Not only do they display a fierce desire to retain total daily control over the retail business, allowing no room for delegation, but their language problems enhance the obvious deficiencies in business awareness. No record of sales was kept in most outlets visited and prices were arrived at on the basis of dividing up the amount on the cash and carry pack and adding a little extra. However, dedication to the job itself could not be criticised. Retailers were motivated usually by a desire to improve their family position and ensure that sufficient funds could be generated to provide a family wedding or improve the son's education. In this sense Jenkins's[6] explanation for ethnic minority participation in small-scale retailing appears to hold true – the 'culture' model which assumes that certain groups have a developed cultural predisposition towards business activities. The cultural predisposition, however, does not equip them with the technical knowledge to run a small retail business more efficiently.

Although most small retail managers/owners are aware that there may be deficiencies in their business operation skills, few can spare the time to obtain the training necessary to remedy the situation. One couple, Dreena and Patrick Hanlon, wished to set up a shop in a rural location.[7] Although they were lucky enough to be able to call on the help of the Rural Development Commission for practical guidance, their circumstances and attitudes typify those of many small shopowners. Patrick had been working in London as an accountant for many years, commuting to and from their Sussex home. Tired with the four-hour train journey he decided they needed a change of direction. Patrick's banking experience meant he wasn't skilled for many other jobs. But retailing is one career which doesn't demand many formal qualifications. Running a village shop appealed to them because they liked living in a small community. They also thought it would be good for their children, Caroline (11) and James (14).

The problem appears to be in detaching the idealistic picture of small-scale retailing from the reality. Dawson alludes to this weakness when he talks of 'inflexible and outdated management techniques' as a reason for decline in small-scale retailing. The response he suggests to the problem is to 'seek advice on store operation management'.[8] In many cases, this is easier said than done due to both financial and, perhaps more importantly, time constraints on the busy retailer. In Case Study B, however, the owner's professional approach to management was clearly a critical factor in the business success.

A recent survey on the 'Reasons for Small Business Failure' sponsored by accountants Stoy Hayward and Nat West Bank[9] looked at the case histories of 437 failed businesses as supplied by just over 200 bank managers. The study stated that, while the key contributory factor in small business failure was financial among businesses in the wholesaling, manufacturing and distribution sectors, it was poor management in the retailing, construction and catering sectors.

Lack of direction

Curran[12] characterises small firms' strategies as resembling a 'spiders web'. 'Decision making is highly centralised with other members of the enterprise often being uncertain about their precise responsibilities or the overall aims of the business'. Another weakness which often accompanies inexperienced management is the fact that, despite the lack of complexity in the smaller business, many seem to lack a clear direction.

Overstocking

The same report highlighted another major weakness amongst small retail businesses, the problem of overstocking. The report states that obsolete products feature both as primary and contributing factors in failures, presumably due to overstocking of products that would not sell. Whether it is four cartons of out-of-date cream, unfashionable jumpers, stale loaves of bread, or a stockroom filled with tins of petfood with a label displaying a dated competition offer, wasted stock equals lost money.

One grocery outlet visited recently displayed the following range of tinned soups – Heinz (large can, 17 varieties; small can, 10 varieties), Campbell's standard and condensed (16 varieties), Baxters (12 varieties) as well as several speciality ranges such as 'Erasio' turtle and brandy. Yet sales of soups averaged only 8 tins per week. The owner of the store was anxious that no customer should come into the store and not be able to find the variety they were looking for. That was an expensive policy decision.

Undoubtedly the marketing strategy of smaller retailers should include the facility to look after local needs, but this must be restricted to a selection of products where there is sufficient demand to make them viable to stock. This problem will be discussed in more depth in chapter 6. Tony Hurran, in the *Independent Grocer*,[10] sums it up, 'it is no use stocking 6 varieties of Old English Mint Imperials simply because three customers purchase one packet each per fortnight and insist on alternating the flavours'.[11] For every slow-moving line on a shelf there are two, three or more quick turnover money spinners waiting to jump into that space. Good space control system are part and parcel of an efficiently-managed retail operation and are as important to travel agents, estate agents, hairdressers as to grocery and fashion outlets.

Legislation

Perhaps the threats and weaknesses which have been most widely documented are those which, again, are largely uncontrollable. *Government legislation* can undoubtedly have an important impact on the success of the small retailer. Most relevant at the time of writing, being the almost inevitable reform of the 1950s, the Shops Act before 1990. Although the British Independent Grocers Association, British Retailers Association and the Community Shop Group were all fighting to restrict the right to open longer hours to shops under 3000 square feet, the pressure from the multiple DIY sector, Asda and Tesco (led by Conservative MP Sir Basil Feldman), combined with the government's stated intention to introduce 'free for all' Sunday trading form powerful opposition. Although general grocery retailers might be adversely affected by multiples trading on Sunday, it is likely that 'specialist' small outlets retailing products like confectionery, speciality cakes and bread, ornaments and jewellery could benefit, particularly if they are sited strategically next to railway stations, in shopping malls or tourist areas, and so on. An increase in the number of stores open on Sunday would undoubtedly have a knock-on effect on associated services with the accompanying potential for retail development.

Small retailers linked with the alcohol industry are optimistically predicting additional sales from the extension of the licensing laws in 1989.

The National Federation of Self-Employed has expressed an anxiety about the effect on the smaller retailer of the reform of the local taxes being introduced in 1990. One area of major concern is the idea that small traders who live above their retail premises might be forced to pay a business rate on their shop *and* a poll tax on the living accommodation above it.

In the current retail climate, no discussion of the potential impact/threat of legislation would be adequate without reference to laws being passed by the machinery of the *European* Parliament. The information relevant to small retail businesses is being dealt with by the Task Force for Small and Medium-Sized Enterprises (SME) whose role is discussed in more depth in the concluding chapter of the book. A few basic ideas need to be mentioned at this stage, however. The smaller retailers' market in the UK is undoubtedly going to be under threat from European operations in the near future. With the aid of computer technology, and the relaxation of trade barriers envisaged by 1992, a small retailer will be able to link the activities of his business across many national boundaries without losing efficiency. The most obvious example of such an operation is the Italian Clothing firm Benetton. Their clothes are made by a host of small suppliers in Italy and sold through 2000 franchised retail outlets throughout Europe and the USA. Benetton provides the designs and controls production based on computerised sales returns from outlets. Benetton is just one example, and other companies will undoubtedly follow their pattern. The example of Benetton again emphasises the importance of franchising as a different mode of operation for the smaller retailer, particularly beneficial if venturing into foreign territory.

Although these legislative changes have been included in the 'threats' section of the analysis, many can equally be viewed as opportunities, particularly those relating to 1992 innovations. However, the smaller firm faces a distinct disadvantage in meeting the plethora of legislation surrounding all business. The larger firm can afford to retain specialist expertise, but the smaller business has to retain an awareness of the importance of a wide range of matters.

The authors have deliberately avoided emphasising the broader economic threats facing the smaller retailer as they have been widely documented elsewhere and again tend to affect the retail sector in general rather than the small retailer specifically, for example, inflation, polarisation of buying points, and changes in consumer spending. Increased operating costs obviously affect the smaller business more harshly. However, although multiples can exploit economies of scale, close cost control and good accounting systems can often offset these disadvantages. The lack of capital for investment is again a wider issue which is frequently cited as a reason for the demise of small retailers. Although government financial assistance does appear to be available (as Curran[13] points out, 'small firms are politically fashionable') there is still some question as to the extent of awareness among retailers of the availability of such state aid.

Location

Finally, the question of location needs to be included as a problem for the smaller retailer. There is the idea that small operators can only afford to locate in areas where the market in the catchment area is insufficient to support the volume of business necessary to survive. In chapter 4 the topic of location is discussed in some detail and the authors put forward some positive ideas about how location can be explored more effectively to the advantage of the smaller retailer.

Keypoint summary

Strengths and opportunities

- Greater accessibility to requirements/needs
- Flexibility
- Diversity of mode of operation, e.g., convenience, franchising
- Potential for greater operational control
- Few barriers to entry
- Government assistance

Weaknesses and threats

- Power of multiples, particularly price competition
- Lack of business acumen
- Tendency to overstock
- National and international legislation
- Increased operating costs
- Lack of capital for investment
- Poor locations

CHAPTER 3

Retail Strategy for the Smaller Business

Most businesses have a clear objective. It might not be posted on a noticeboard or even at the front of every employee's mind. But the objective is obvious enough; to improve last year's sales and profit performance.

The problem is rarely to set an objective, because such objectives set themselves and will be all too obvious to the independent business person. The problem is usually how to achieve the objective.

If defining an objective sets the direction, a business strategy explains how a company can achieve its goal. Strategy is rarely quantifiable. It is not concerned so much with *what* is sold but *how* it is sold. It is not the ability to define the profitability of a business but more whether the business can make a profit. In fact, understanding why an existing business is or is not profitable is essential to managing that business in the long term.

Words such as strategy and objectives might appear irrelevant to the independent business. They are not. Too many small businesses fail because their owners do not recognise that their business strategy is flawed. In retailing too many are knowingly or otherwise competing on price with the larger multiples, a sure fire recipe for failure in the majority of circumstances.

In developing a strategy for the independent we need to first trace the rise in multiple power and to explore the lessons for the independent sector.

The rise in multiple power

Until the turn of the twentieth century, the independent retailer had only other, similar-sized, companies to fear.[1] Many retailers were still craft retailers, specialising in one product type. They were manufacturers as well as retailers, converting raw materials into saleable items in their own back-rooms. The idea of serving an apprenticeship as a shop assistant was still valid, such was the specialist nature of many trades.

Between 1900 and the Second World War we saw a change in retailing that reflected in its magnitude the industrial revolution of a century or more before. The retail revolution was caused in part by the changes wrought by the changes in the manufacturing sector. Mass production had made consumer goods cheaper to make. Employment in the mass production industries gave a broad range of the population a real increase in disposable income. Workers, including a growing number of female employees, could now aspire to the manufactured goods that had once been the preserve of the middle class.

Mass production caused prices to fall. On top of this, British exports of manufactured goods were paid for by imports of cheap food at prices low enough to undercut that produced locally.

The retail business which had relied upon a considerable expertise in local purchasing and manufacturing found itself competing with cheaper imports and mass-produced merchandise. Control over the retail market-place began to slip from the small shop into the hands of wholesalers who could co-ordinate the distribution of both imported goods and British goods alike. Wholesalers replaced the retailer as packagers of many of these products. At the same time manufacturers began to use the new mass media to extol the virtues of guaranteed quality and low prices inherent in their offerings.

Both trends served to reduce the skills needed by the retailer in offering goods to customers. On the surface this may not seem to have posed a threat to the typical retailer. The change might have been welcomed as an opportunity to concentrate on selling to the customer rather than on making or preparing the goods. However, the advantages of economies of scale were also being recognised by a growing number of retail multiples.

In 1900 the proportion of all retail sales accounted for by the multiples with ten or more outlets was only some 3 to $4\frac{1}{2}$ per cent.[2] One advantage of the multiple that threatened the independent retailer was purchasing power. Such is the pressure on any business to achieve enough volume to break even, before it is possible to make a profit, that a large order from a multiple at a reduced price was always attractive. The multiple could and did choose to pass on some or all of the price advantage gained by bulk buying in lower prices to consumers. Inevitably this meant greater sales and even greater negotiating power for the manufacturers.

In many countries, and also in Britain, the consequences of a totally free market in distributing consumer goods were felt to be undesirable. Smaller retailers, it was argued, would be unable to compete. They would cease trading and their going would be felt most by the country dweller and anyone else unable to shop conveniently at one of a limited number of multiple outlets.

The result was Resale Price Maintenance (RPM), first as a voluntary arrangement and then imposed by statute. Retailers were barred from reducing their prices below those set by the manufacturer or wholesaler. Manufacturers, not surprisingly, were often avid supporters of RPM as the protection afforded to the independent retailer extended to their own margins.

Despite RPM the larger multiples continued to gain ground. Their economies of scale were not limited to those obtained through bulk buying. Own-label merchandise did not fall under the scope of RPM. Trading stamps offered a more direct circumvention of price control, so did free delivery or loss leading on merchandise not controlled by RPM.

In 1964 RPM was abolished on virtually every product item. Small retailers soon found themselves buying from wholesalers at prices often barely below those offered to the public by the larger retailers.

Greater concentration amongst the multiples and greater centralisation of buying in the 1970s and 1980s saw the emergence of a limited number of major retailers in each market; Sainsbury, Tesco, Asda,

Dee and Argyll in food; MFI and Harris in furniture; Boots in chemists; W H Smith and Menzies in stationery; Burton, Marks and Spencer, BHS and Sears in fashion and so on.

The multiples had gained their dominance in the retail market place mainly through their inherent price advantage, but by the 1980s even the largest recognised that continuing to compete on price alone with each other was unlikely to be sustainable as a strategy. With none of the larger players holding a significant economic advantage, price competition would inevitably lead to falling margins.[3]

Image emerged as a major weapon in retailer competition in the 1980s. The more successful of the new retail entrants, and Next would be the most obvious of examples, often used image as their prime strategy.

Competitive strategy

Up until the 1980s larger retailers used their scale economies to grow at the expense of the independent and co-operative sectors. In the jargon of the corporate strategist, price was their main competitive advantage. The brief history of retailing at the beginning of this chapter is included to make two points: the price advantage of the multiple, and the use of image by even the strongest of multiples to avoid competing solely on price amongst themselves. In these two points lies the key to a successful retail strategy for the smaller business; to avoid competing on price with the multiples and instead to use image to advantage, not only as a weapon against the multiples, but against other, similar-sized retail operations.

The idea of avoiding price competition does not mean that price is irrelevant in retailing. No business can survive for long if its customers see it as expensive. However, those same customers will not begrudge paying more if they believe they receive something extra for a higher price. They will argue that they are getting 'value for money' rather than a 'low price'. The two phrases mean totally different things in the customer's mind. Value for money is often used as a label to describe a situation where a person pays more than is absolutely necessary but does not feel cheated.

Applying theory to practice

The basis of competitive strategy is to develop a number of points of difference between a business and its competitors.[4] These strategic planks must be valued by customers and drive the business as a whole. The smaller retailer seems to have three main options in selecting the planks to support a thriving business, building on the strengths illustrated in chapter 2.

The three planks are product specialisation, service and location. Some retailers can succeed by combining elements of all three, all small retailers will fail eventually unless at least one is applied to good effect.

Product specialisation

The smaller retailer can succeed by developing an expertise in depth in a single product or narrow product range. Sock Shop, Tie Rack and Bodyshop all represent companies that have grown significantly on the basis of offering not totally unique products, but a specialist range that can be offered to the customer with authority. Another example is Health Foods and associated products in case study B on the Happy Nut House at the end of this book.

Sometimes product specialisation can be very narrow. A number of shops exist who carry only buttons. Some specialise in very large size shoes, one or two in clogs, some in trophies, some in silk bridal wear. The list of possibilities is enormous, but there are two constraints on any strategy based solely on the product being sold.

The first constraint is the total market demand for the chosen product. The demand can be both too low or too high. Too low and the business fails through lack of turnover, too high and the innovative idea can be exploited by the multiples who represent the second constraint. The case study at the end of this book on Health Food Retailing illustrates this point well in that as demand for 'healthier' foods grew, so did the interest of the likes of Boots and Tesco. However, the examples of Sock Shop and Tie Rack illustrate that fast expansion by the innovator can pre-empt any competitive response. Both companies chose to grow quickly to satisfy the market demand nationally, and at the same time develop the necessary economies of scale to fight the larger stores on price, if necessary. Once established, flexibility and the ability to change would hold the keys to success.

Service

Retailing is the largest part of the service sector of the economy. That said, the level of service offered by many stores leaves much to be desired. The potential to generate competitive advantage through better service has been recognised by the largest retailers who have invested heavily in customer-care programmes.

In the 1930s, when unemployment was high and labour costs were falling, retailers used service as a key marketing weapon. It is likely that the same high level of unemployment in the 1980s has something to do with a similar trend today.

Advertising by retailers who seek to improve our perception of their service levels offer some clues as to our views on the service we receive. A leading bank, for example, contrasted the structured, impersonal approach of their competitors with what they saw as their own more open, friendly and personalised service. People it seems prefer to be treated as individuals rather than as account numbers.

Service extends beyond customer service, or recognising customers as people, it also encompasses expertise. Despite the improvement in quality of the meat offer in supermarkets, many shoppers prefer to patronise their local butcher.[5] As one housewife explained 'He knows what I want and I can trust him. If I 'phone through an order and pick it up on the way home, he insists on showing me the meat before it is finally packed'.

A shoe shop in South Manchester specialised in children's shoes. A full range of two leading brands was stocked. Each child was measured, no exceptions were made. When the selection was made the owner/manager had to approve the fit before a sale was made. Parents who wanted a faster service or children who wanted a particular style that did not fit correctly were firmly put in their place. The shop gained a reputation for its expertise in fitting children's shoes, and as many parents believed not only in caring for their children's feet but also that their offspring possessed uniquely shaped feet, the store prospered.

The extended hours of convenience stores and many shops operated by Asian retailers such as that in Case Study A at the end of the book offer another method of competing on service.

Small shops are often convenient shops. They are just around the corner and their opening hours are more flexible than those of their multiple competitors. Being 'open all hours' can put a strain on the owner/manager and any family concerned with the business but such a strategy has been a particularly profitable one. Convenience stores have prospered next door to a superstore by catering for the customer who chooses not to spend an hour shopping for just one or two items.

Location

Very few stores have no competition to speak of, but some village stores come quite close to this idyllic situation. Granted the total market being served may be highly limited, but serving a local community's needs across a wide range of products can be financially rewarding. Such opportunities are few and far between. The age of mass transportation means that most households can travel more than a few miles with some ease. However, a substantial minority of households do not enjoy the use of a car during the working day. One voluntary chain of grocers found that their typical customer travelled less than a mile to shop with them, did not have the use of a car, shopped frequently and did not hold a large stock of food.[6]

The importance of location is further developed in a later chapter. For the purpose of this section location offers the third method of differentiating one retailer from another that can be used to good effect by the independent retailer.

Combined strategies

The Tie Rack were mentioned as an example of product specialisation earlier on. Their policies on location were also important in differentiating their offer from those of their competitors. Many of their sites were located on railway stations and at airports. Not only did this approach bring their merchandise to the notice of customers who might not have shopped regularly at all, it also made it difficult for any customer to make a comparison with possibly similar merchandise in a high street store.

A garden centre is an example of combining product specialisation with convenience in location and advice on a favourite pastime for many Britons. However, combinations of strategies must offer some synergy rather than blurring the clear image that the independent retailer must seek to present. The personality of any business is as complex as the personality of any individual person and yet, to extend the analogy, to trust any one we seem to need to obtain a clear picture of that person. A confused business image or an incoherent one causes confusion and even mistrust as we fail to perceive a clear picture of what that business is about.

Supporting the chosen strategy

The purpose of a strategy is to differentiate the business, and unless it has an economic advantage, isolate it from competing solely on price with other, similar business. A successful strategy is not, even so, a guarantee of commercial success as the business must be run efficiently. Nevertheless, a valid strategy is a starting point that should not be ignored.

Responsibility for defining a strategic direction for a business of any size rests with the most senior of management. In larger businesses it may well be significant that companies with valid strategies are often run by individuals with a strong or even dominant personality of their own. Simon Marks is often credited with laying much of the foundations for Marks and Spencer.[7] A half-century later and Next, shaped by George Davies, was being hailed as a threat to Britain's largest retail operation. The Sainsbury family have always been closely involved with the business that bears their name. Terence Conran and Ralph Halpern are two more names that spring to mind for their abilities to act as figure heads in guiding retail businesses and in reshaping them.

The value of one person with an original concept with the power to control and refine the developing business has been noted as a common factor in the personal and business careers of a number of self-made tycoons, a number of whom being retailers.[8]

The larger the business the more difficult it becomes for a single individual to impose his or her will on the operation. A small business, by contrast, could find it easier to follow the clear lead of one person. Retailing, it is said with some justification, is about change. The literature on the management of change is full of references to the need for a senior manager to act as the agent of change by championing any innovation. Changing the direction of a company would require the champion to be the most senior executive, which in the case of a small business will be the owner.

As will be shown later in chapter 9 on The People Dimension, the owner's management style will be a vital factor in defining and, more so, in implementing a business strategy. Many of the successful retail personalities are or have been regarded somewhat as autocrats, but the success of the business they run may well require more than just an element of the dictator!

Cost control and price leadership

A good image will keep the customers coming into a store, but the profits will depend just as much on the control of net margin. While the generalisation on cost leadership for the smaller retailer as a dangerous strategy is perfectly valid, there are some exceptions to that rule. It is worth then spending some time examining cost and price issues from a strictly strategic perspective before dismissing the idea of price as being totally irrelevant at this level.

The basic economic reasons why a small retailer cannot use low price as a central plank in defining its overall competitive position are the absence of economies of scale and the presence of fixed costs (rent, rates, fixturing), and variable costs (stock, staff) that cannot be reduced to levels possible for the multiple retailer. There are, however, certain trading formats which allow the smaller business to reduce or even eliminate some of its cost burdens.

Cost-based strategies

A market stall attracts few costs in terms of fixturing. Rent and rates are replaced by an often nominal sum for a pitch. Trading is normally limited to one day a week, a day which is well known locally. This tends to concentrate customer flow on that day with only the vagaries of the weather to contend with as a major threat. It is interesting to see fixed shops adjacent to a market-place closing their doors on market days and even moving their merchandise onto a market stall, such is the strength of the image that markets have in offering the customer competitive prices.

Another retail format that does allow the smaller business to compete on price is direct response via mail order or direct selling. Selling directly to the end customer does not incur the overheads of a shop and the economies of scale only start to accrue at a much higher level of turnover. The novel idea or the small specialist product could be eminently suited to this type of retailing and the retailer could be well placed to sell on price, whether the retailer would be well advised to is a different matter entirely.

The approaches of a market stall, the allied format of street trading and direct response selling are probably the only formats offering the smaller retailer the potential for an economic advantage over the larger multiple. However, none guarantee such an advantage over a rival who offers the same merchandise in the same way to the same customers. Yet, again, the retailer has only image as a weapon to avoid debilitating price competition with someone against whom there is no economic advantage.

Cost control

The reader will have gained the impression that there is little potential or value for most smaller retailers to use price at all in business. While this is true at the strategic level, it is not the situation at the operational level. Control over costs to keep prices down and margins up is central to success in any business. Some costs such as rent, rates and fitments cannot be controlled. They can be negotiated at one point in time but other than that they are outside of the retailer's control. Costs due to staff and stock are by contrast capable of detailed appraisal.

The proportion of total costs represented by staff costs varies depending upon the business, but can represent up to one-third of turnover. It follows that net profit can be highly dependent upon the level of staff costs. Many small retailers minimise their apparent wage costs through the long hours worked by their owner/managers or their families. Many more use part-time staff astutely to ensure staff are available when the business requires their presence rather than all day, irrespective of the level of customer traffic.

The potential to reduce staff costs also exists wherever labour can be eliminated by automation. Retailing is a relatively labour intensive business but one where labour cannot easily be replaced by a machine. The smaller retailer may in turn have to rely upon offering high service to compete and service levels are generally concerned with people. Electronic point of sale (EPOS) can offer the potential to reduce activities such as stock-taking and price marking, but there are no known alternatives for the human shelf-stacker or sales assistant.

Some service retailers may be able to automate some traditionally human activities. Travel agents can use telephone access to computer data bases rather than telephone calls or using directories. Manual filing systems in a car repair or spare part business can be placed onto microfiche. Computers can be used to print out instructions for use on pharmaceuticals dispensed by a chemist. Electronic mail can be used to communicate between stores in a voluntary association such as Interflora. At the end of the day the savings are usually finite and measurable, if not as obvious as one might hope.

Price promotion

The issue of price as a promotional and in other words tactical weapon in retail competition is considered later in the book, suffice it to say for the moment that giving special offers, holding an annual sale, or selling loss leaders as a method of generating interest and traffic is not the same as gearing the whole business to compete on price. The smallest shop can benefit from cutting the price of a limited number of staple items every so often to give the impression of being worth dropping into for such offers and of competing where possible with the larger shops. Grocery stores use the technique of cutting prices on so-called Known Value Items (KVIs) to achieve this end. The equivalent of butter and sugar in a grocers might be a pair of tights in a ladies wear shop or a tin of white gloss paint in an ironmongers. The item will sell well and could even be regarded as making a net profit as an individual line, but this is not the objective. The trick here seems to be to be seen to offer a competitive price while not having to achieve price equality across the full range of products on offer.

The dual effect of own-label merchandise

The growth in own-label merchandise has been one of the features of the retail scene in recent years. In some retail sectors such as shoes the retailers' brands dominate the market. In others such as toys and pharmaceuticals, branded merchandise still retains its pre-eminence.

The reasons for retailers offering own-label are various but two elements predominate. Own-label helps the retailer establish its own differentiated identity as part of a product specialisation strategy. Own-label products also support any price leadership strategy because margins are generally higher, in the absence of the manufacturer's promotional costs. It is also more difficult for the customer to compare prices on non-branded items.

The emphasis until recently in many retail sectors was to concentrate on the price aspects of own-label merchandise. Some quite enormous price cuts below branded product prices were commonplace. Unfortunately quality in many instances was highly variable and often poor. Gradually retailers recognised the damage such product offers did to their overall image and began to emphasise value and quality rather than mere price.

Such an approach to own-labelling, or what is now better called own-branding, has its consequences particularly in quality control and in the technical expertise retained by the retailer.[9] The impetus for monitoring quality must stem from the retailer for own-brand merchandise. After all, the manufacturer has less to lose when it is the retailer's name on the label than when it is their own if the customer is dissatisfied.

Smaller retailers are often reluctant to enter the own-label arena because of the setting-up costs and the extra responsibilities involved, but even the smallest of stores can look to a limited range of goods under their own name. The local grocer can become renowned for its home-cooked hams and cakes; the menswear shop for a range of ties that are their own design; the travel agent for a package holiday that they themselves put together – each can enhance both margin and image. Alternatively, some wholesalers[10] offer a range of own brand to the independent and most voluntary chains specialise in doing so.

So what is image?

The image of a retail store has been defined as the blend of tangible and intangible elements that combine to produce the way the typical customer perceives the given outlet.[11] Various views exist on what are the major elements that create store image. Figure 3.1 lists the kind of factors that, arguably, contribute to a retail image.

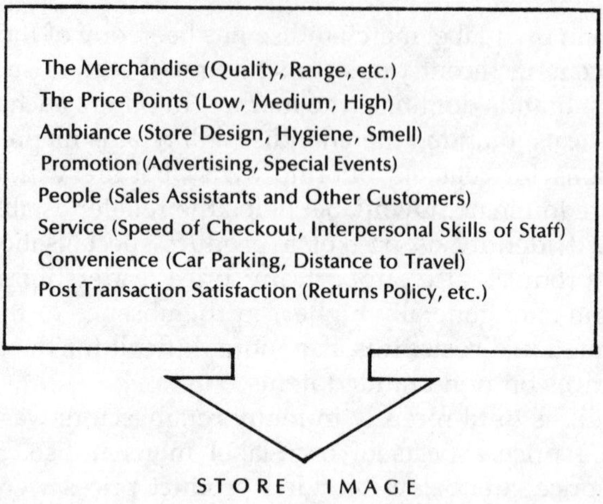

Figure 3.1 Elements of a retail image

The one area that does appear to be questionable in the creation of a retail image is advertising.[12] This needs some explanation as advertising is clearly of use in the creation and promotion of an image for a branded product.

The evidence for and against the value of advertising in creating a store image is unfortunately limited to data on multiple retailers. Tesco is a good example of a retailer who changed from a 'pile it high, sell it cheap' philosophy to one based more on large, well-presented stores and quality own-label merchandise. As their image moved so their advertising budget was cut. Next represents one of the more image-led retailers but the metamorphosis of Hepworth as Next was achieved with a minimal advertising budget. Marks and Spencer, BHS and John Lewis partnership have all achieved a strong image without the benefit of advertising. The Co-op and Woolworth have been two of the heaviest of advertisers. Woolworth advertising has won prizes for creativity but advertising has not been successful in repositioning either store.

Only MFI and KwikSave have been successful in promoting what is for both a price-led image using advertising and it is in price-led retailing that advertising seems to work best. Advertising is covered in a later chapter as part of promotion for the smaller company, but suffice it to say that advertising, on its own at least, will not create an image for a store. What seems to happen is that a good advertisement extolling the virtues of shopping at a particular store will even backfire on the retailer if the store does not live up to the image being promoted, more of this in a moment, but the role of advertising seems limited to announcing and informing about the shop rather than anything more creative. It is not surprising that most retail advertising is in the printed media rather than on television.

The evidence suggests that store design and layout are the equivalent of advertising in retailing with advertising playing a supporting rather than a leading role.

The financial value of image

Figure 3.2 sums up the potential for a 'good' image to affect the trade of a retailer of any size. Image can be described as an attitude which in turn is a predisposition to react in a certain way to a stimulus. In the context of this book the stimulus is a retail offer, and the relevant attitude the image held of the retailer's offer by its customers and potential customers. A change to a more favourable image of the shop and more customers come in. They spend more per visit and tend to purchase more, higher margin products. Image is therefore central in attracting customers and in converting a visit into expenditure. A retailer's image is also the way the customer perceives the retailer's strategy.

Conversely the opposite is true when a store has a poor image or an incoherent image as illustrated in Figure 3.3. Customers tend not to visit the shop. If they do, they spend very little and many leave

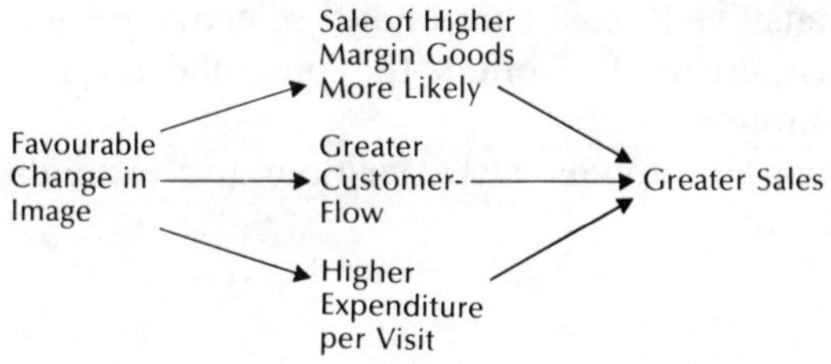

Figure 3.2 The positive effects of image

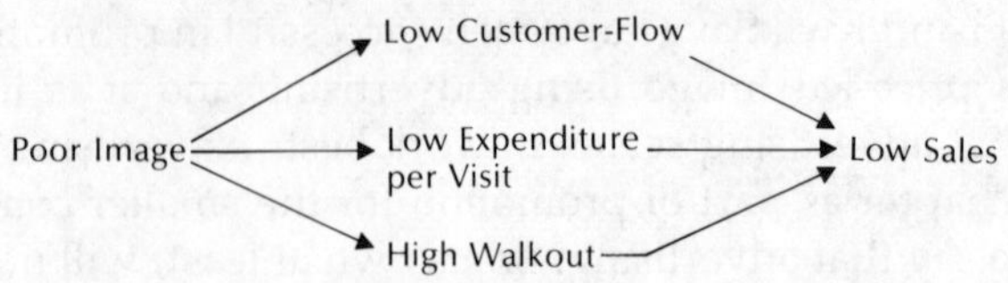

Figure 3.3 The problems caused by a poor image

without buying. The last group: those who are categorised as 'walkouts', are in many ways the most interesting to concentrate on when identifying image problems with a shop. They have, after all, been attracted into the shop but have possibly been disappointed by the offer inside the store. Put another way, the internal delivery did not match the external image. This can happen as explained earlier if a retailer attempts to create an image that the store cannot live up to.

Figure 3.2 sums up this chapter on Retail Strategy. Any shop needs an image that helps it maximise customer-flow and sales per customer. A good image or a good strategy is one that differentiates the shop from its competitors, allowing it to avoid price competition and stimulate the customer because it is different. Creating the right image and maintaining it is a major theme throughout the rest of this book.

Keypoint summary

1. Multiple retailers have grown since 1900 because of their inherent cost and price advantages over the independent sector.
2. In the 1980s even the multiples have moved to non-price competition recognising their lack of any economic advantage in competing with one another.
3. Three non-price bases for competition appear open to the independent sector: product specialisation, service and location.
4. A few smaller retailers can use price as a competitive strategy, all must be sensitive to cost control and selective price promotion.
5. Own-label merchandise offers the potential for both price and image promotion.
6. A good image promotes customer-flow and expenditure and reduces walkouts.

CHAPTER 4

Location Decisions

The old addage has it, reputedly from Colonel Sanders, that there are only three important factors in retailing: location, location and location. BP's Richard Jungins has a slightly different law for his Food Plus Convenience outlets, 'location, location and operation are the golden rules'. A number of exceptions in the multiple sector to these apparent rules, such as Habitat and Argos, who prosper from what are regarded as often secondary sites, may call into question the generalisation that location is all-important. However, the amount of care taken by leading food multiples in site assessment would indicate that where a retail business *is* can be as important as what it *does*.

Analytical techniques

A number of sophisticated modelling techniques exist to help guide retailers on location decisions.[1] These fall into two basic types: gravity models and forecasting models. A gravity model assumes that the ability of a store to attract customers increases with the size of the shopping centre of which the store forms a part, and decreases with the distance the customer has to travel to the centre, as the inverse of the distance travelled to that centre. As a formula:

$$\text{Probability of visiting the store} \propto \frac{\text{Size of centre}}{\text{Distance to the centre}}$$

Unfortunately for the smaller retailer, even one with a degree in mathematics, the equations that can be employed to any practical effect are relatively complex and require a good deal of empirical data to solve. The general principle of gravity models is nevertheless fundamental to good decision-making and this is the importance of the pulling power of a retail centre as opposed to a single shop. Unless the retailer is so specialised that its offer alone can pull customers to it, each shop is dependent upon the collective pulling power of every other shop in its location.

A second type of model that is used by the multiple sector is the regression type. It is clear that a number of factors can affect the customer traffic that any store could expect in a new location. A retailer with a large number of shops could construct a model for customer-flow or average takings in this form:

$$\text{Sales} = A - B \times \textit{no. of competitors} + C \times \textit{population} + \textit{etc.}$$

where *A*, *B* and *C* are unknown constants.

By measuring each factor, number of competitors, size of population and so on, for each existing store in a chain, the various unknown in the equation (*A*, *B*, *C*, etc.) can be calculated using multiple regression. Again, the level of sophistication is impractically high for most independent retailers but the principle behind the idea is relevant. There are a number of factors that can and should be assessed before making a location decision.

A checklist for location

Views differ on the importance of individual factors and the relevance of each to any particular type of retailer, so, in no particular order, these are the factors most often cited as important to consider in any location decision.

The size of the population in the local area

The nature of that population
The strength of competition
The number of people passing the site
The available parking
The quality of public transport
The visibility of the site
Factors affecting future potential
Ability to expand the shop physically
The nature of any legal agreements
The site costs

Many individuals are attracted to the idea of owning and operating their own businesses. Managing a shop is one of the more popular. The mistake most frequently made by such individuals is to ignore the trade-off between the pulling power of the site and its cost. A site is often cheap for no other reason than because it is not an attractive proposition.

A few retail formats can trade quite effectively from secondary sites. Such retailers include many who sell a service, such as travel, insurance and hairdressing, or where the purchase is infrequent such as furniture. All such retailers have one thing in common, and that is the purchase situation is not routine and is often planned in isolation from other shopping trips.

Once attracting casual custom from the passing trade becomes important, then a location in the heart of a busy centre becomes more important, even a necessity.

Anchor stores and malls

Shopping centres often depend upon anchor stores. Marks and Spencer in Britain would be a prime example as would a number of department stores in the USA. People will plan their shopping expeditions around the presence of such stores and talk about 'visiting Macclesfield because it's got a Marks while Wilmslow hasn't'.

In France a number of the larger food retailers trade as hypermarkets with half or more of their footage given over to non-foods. They are often in satellite shopping areas quite distant from the town and enjoy substantial car parking, and can attract visitors from considerable distances. Their importance to the smaller retailer is that they often sublet small units not only within the store as concessions, but also in small malls at the front of the store. In Britain the idea has not yet taken hold although it is interesting to see Asda moving in that general direction at the time of writing.

Many department stores offer concession areas to smaller shops.

DIY stores may contain the odd kitchen concession and a double-glazing display. For the smaller retailer, especially a company who are primarily a manufacturer looking for an outlet for their goods under their own control, the idea can be attractive. Some large retailers do seem to be having second thoughts about the value to them of concessions. Debenhams are one to have reduced the total number of concessions, albeit to be replaced by other offers from within the Burton group. The problem for the larger host store is to keep control over its own image with a collection of concessions all of whom are primarily concerned with their own image and performance.

The issue is basically one of compatibility and this works both ways. The host will not be too pleased with any activities by the concession that detract from their own business while the concession has to rely upon the host for its customer flow. Any retailer considering a potential host must obtain detailed information on the number and type of customer the host attracts. There is little point setting up in a store who cater for a totally different customer profile.

Covered malls

Many retail innovations begin in the United States. In location terms the most significant trend has been the covered mall. The typical American mall is located in the suburbs, has substantial parking, a number of anchor stores (normally department stores) and one or more central features ranging from fountains and fast-food restaurants to swimming pools and other leisure facilities. The development of retail malls began only in the 1960s, but by the 1980s over a third of all retail sales were achieved in such centres. The rate of growth in new developments has slackened considerably as many areas have become overfooted. A study by one of the authors comparing the Philadelphia and Greater Manchester areas in 1987 indicated that there was twice the footage per head of population in the American conurbation compared to that in Manchester. Even allowing for the higher disposable income in America (in real terms probably only 30 per cent) the difference in floor space is remarkable.

One other issue apparent from studying American malls is that customers appear to be loyal to malls, sometimes at the expense of their store loyalty. The responsibility for attracting customers is after all a joint one, as the retailer will often pay rent or management fees to the mall developers. In some instances that rent paid is proportional to the turnover of the store and if the store does not achieve what is regarded as an acceptable turnover, the retailer is obliged to move out.

The retailer's identity is in many ways subsumed within the identity of the mall. In many instances this tendency is enhanced by the homogeneous architectural style of the mall itself. Shoppers comment that they are often unsure which of the large anchor stores in the mall they are actually in at any one time.

American malls have also been criticised for destroying the downtown or city centre areas. Stores have closed as shoppers see little reason in struggling through crowded roads to the antiquated facilities in the centre of town, when they can drive in comfort to a pleasant environment in the suburbs.

Changes in planning philosophy

In the past local authorities have taken substantial powers in deciding on new retail developments. An important concept has been the protection of the existing status quo on the grounds, for example, that new developments endanger city centres and that adequate provision should preclude any additional development. The situation in Britain is not as bureaucratic as in some parts of Europe where large-scale development has been barred by fears of over-development and the consequences of too much competition. Nevertheless, planning applications for new stores and out-of-town retail centres have often taken years to be accepted with developers being asked to fund often unrelated projects such as new swimming baths and motorway extensions as sops to local planning committees.

Clarification in 1988 of the powers of planning authorities, including a clear directive that adequate existing provision cannot be used to deny an application, seemed to open the way to an increase in retail floor space, much of which was to be on new out-of-town sites adjacent to motorway systems such as the M25 in the south-east and the M63 in the north-west.

Two factors therefore that will be important to the independent retailer in the future are: the potential for increased competition as local authorities are unable to use the presence of similar retail outlets to deny a new application, and the need to consider taking space in out-of-town malls.

Independent retailers are rarely seen in the newer malls which appear to attract the multiples, but it is here that the future lies for retailers of all types and size.

Lease or purchase decisions

High Street rents and rates have increased well ahead of inflation in most parts of Britain. Independent retailers trading in city or town centres tend to rent rather than purchase their premises. A critical document that can affect both short- and long-term profitability is the lease. The independent business has to rely upon outside legal advice from solicitors or estate agents in negotiating a lease, or is well advised to do so rather than rely upon common sense in deciphering a lease agreement.

One common issue between landlord and tenant, for example, is what constitutes an 'improvement' to the property. Most leases for small premises are for five years these days, down from the 10- or 20-year leases that were common in the 1950s. The landlord and tenant must agree on a new rental at the end of each lease period and the maxim of a fair market value is used to define the new sum. As prices have accelerated under the pressure of expanding retail sales, in an era of restriction on new development, the new rental is generally far higher than the old rental scaled up on an index of inflation. The retailer must ensure that any improvements to the premises are excluded from the reassessment of rental, an obvious point perhaps, but an illustration of the pitfalls for the unwary tenant.

One answer to any potential dispute on lease agreements is to purchase the property outright in the first place. In some instances this will be impossible or impractical. In all cases it ties up capital that could be a valuable source of liquid assets in expanding the business. However, for many single shopkeepers the increase in the value of freehold premises represents a substantial source of profit.

One retailer in Runcorn bought a disused car showroom and converted it into a convenience store.[2] As the business grew, and his own ambitions with it, he built onto the original premises. Over a ten-year period an initial investment of £40 000 grew to be worth £250 000. If Inflation is assumed at 10 per cent compound, the £40 000 investment would have been worth only £104 000. The increase in capital value was worth £15 000 per annum, probably more than the net wage the owner paid himself.

The taxation position on selling a business is not totally straightforward but there are generous capital gains exemptions for a smaller business that is sold up on the retirement of the owner.[3] Taking these into consideration, the attraction of purchasing retail property is obvious. Unfortunately there are two factors that might depress property prices in the future. The first is the potential explosion of retail selling space as the pressure from developers mounts in what could well be an era of relatively light restriction by planning authorities. The second is the standard business rate payable under the switch from rates to the more uniform Community Charge and Business Rate from 1990.

The present principle of rating business property takes account of the market rental for that property. The uniform Business Rate would seem to emphasise the reality that a business wherever it is within a local authority area receives a similar service. Property values in some areas will rise while in others they will fall as the new system is phased in. Doubtless modifications will be needed to the system as proposed at the time of writing, but the general principles are likely to be immutable.

A location niche?

Much of this book is concerned with the concept that competition with the major multiples on price is to be avoided by the independent shopkeeper. Instead the smaller business should seek a highly-differentiated niche. The previous chapter identified three platforms for competing – product specialisation, service and location – that can each be used to differentiate the smaller retailer.

The village shop is an easy example to cite where location is the reason for commercial success. However, general stores have survived and prospered by being close to a multiple competitor rather than far away. One of the Co-op's Late Late Supershop convenience stores was located next door to a large Sainsbury.[4] People used the Supershop for a limited purchase because they saw it as more convenient to use than its larger, probably cheaper competitor. In addition, the convenience store carried items not stocked by the supermarkets such as magazines and videos.

A number of retailers have chosen highly-protected locational niches. The shop in the foyer of the large hotel, the sports shop run by the golf professional at the local course, the school tuck-shop, Tie Rack on railway stations; all these are examples of locating a store near people and conveniently away from other retailers.

Most multiples prefer to locate not only in centres of a particular size but also close to good road access to reduce delivery costs and travel times for area management. Centres catering for 10 000 to 20 000 people are often ignored by the larger companies as being potentially marginal locations, yet the same sites can be a goldmine for the independent.

Speciality locations

Many innovative shops have been launched around a limited range of highly unusual merchandise; china dolls, balloons, Japanese clothing, exotic underwear, hand-painted decoy ducks, self-design T-shirts, dried flower arrangements and other examples of product specialisation. Few shoppers plan to purchase a helium balloon or a T-shirt they design themselves but all of us can be encouraged to browse around a collection of such shops.

A number of centres have been established in many cities as speciality shopping centres. Examples include Covent Garden Market in London, the Corn Exchange in Leeds and the Gardens in Manchester. Many are imaginative conversations of buildings used previously for totally different purposes. Some combine retail and business suites in the same building.

The advantages for the retailer include often tiny sites that can suit the smaller, speciality operator, and promotion by the centre itself as a place to come and browse. On the downside rents can be high and some reports imply considerable difficulties in building traffic into a new location. Special events such as open-air concerts, Punch and Judy shows and personality promotions, none of them without cost, seem essential in encouraging people to spend enough time to also spend their money.

Assessing the local environment

The checklist of factors cited earlier in this chapter included three that were concerned with the size and nature of the local population and their use of shopping facilities. In theory the retailer can estimate the size of a potential business by calculating how much the local community will spend on products that will be sold and estimating the share that the new business could expect to take. Except in extreme cases of, for example estimating the needs of a few households in an isolated corner of the Scottish Highlands, such an approach is unlikely to be totally valid. A better idea is a count of the number of people passing the site and an assessment of whether the local area would patronise the kind of retail offer being considered.

A delicatessen may work well in an up-market suburb but fail in the middle of a council estate. A DIY outlet could be viable in a new estate where young couples are setting up home on tight budgets but fail if the area is mainly rented accommodation.

In essence we are talking about identifying whether a target market exists for the chosen retail format or not. Traditionally such assessments were made using demographic data such as age, family size and social class. Unfortunately for the marketeer many of these measures have declined in efficiency. For example, two of the largest so called socio-economic groups, the largely clerical C_1 and the skilled manual C_2 groups have tended to merge in their purchasing behaviour. Most family units today include more than one wage-earner, and there will be a growing tendency for the female partner in a relationship to account for more than half the income of a couple. The growth in single-person households and single-parent families offer more evidence for the declining relevance of traditional methods of market segmentation.

A number of new methods based upon life-style have considerable potential. One of direct relevance to store location is type of housing. The ACORN system (ACORN stands for A Classification of Residential Neighbourhoods) is used currently by multiple retailers to classify neighbourhoods. The problem yet again for the smaller business is the cost of using such a system, but gradually the typology of every area will become better known and cheaper to obtain.

Life-style

Life-style as a marketing concept is much talked about but rarely defined. Large retailers such as Habitat, Next and Laura Ashley offer practical examples of the somewhat ethereal idea. All three sell a range of co-ordinated products across a broad range of merchandise to certain types of people. These types can be described in traditional demographic terms but each of us can move too easily between life-style concepts for any one to be capable of definition as a customer stereotype. A family may well have a Laura Ashley lounge, a Habitat kitchen and a daughter who seems to spend most of her disposable income at Next. The life-style concept is probably most use to the retailer as a method of co-ordinating a range of product offers in a coherent way so that any customer has a clear idea of what to expect from the store.

Future trends

The independent retailer is often left with very little in the way of formal data of direct use on each locality. Large volumes of information are certainly available. Local media, for example, are an excellent source of statistical data. Studying such information will provide a feel for the area in general terms, but until data such as

ACORN is more widely available it is unlikely that a formal analysis of published data can offer more than a broad brush to aid the location decision.

If the area looks right and the available statistics infer that the local population are likely to appreciate the proposed retail offer, possibly the most important consideration is the change that can be expected in that situation in future years.

A new housing estate presents opportunities for DIY and Garden Centre outlets. A baby shop could do well initially, but unless the population turns over quickly, or building continues, the longer-term potential could be less attractive. A car spares shop can boom in an area where young people are keen on repairing their own vehicles, but do less well as the age profile rises and the same people can afford to pay a garage to maintain their cars.

Large changes in purchasing patterns can occur over as little as ten years. These can be accelerated by new housing and by new roads easing access to other retail centres. Retailers and, in particular, smaller retailers have to evolve with the communities they serve but often fail to do so. Sometimes quite drastic change is called for, the example of the baby shop would be highly relevant. It may be necessary for such a business to change to teenage fashion or to move to another area if the retailer relies upon local patronage.

Expand or multiply

As already stated, the authors recognise that some small businesses want to remain small, others would prefer to grow. Some owners have left well-paid jobs in multiple retailers to 'do their own thing' or to manage something more handleable. Whatever the motives of the owner, if the business succeeds the decision will have to be taken to grow or to restrain the business to a lower level of turnover than might be possible.

If expansion is the chosen pathway, the location decision that must be made is whether to physically build onto the existing shop or buy or lease a second site. The attractions of expanding the existing premises are clear; the staff overhead can be held down, the business is hardly more difficult to control. The alternative, of a second site, requires delegation of at least part of the responsibility for management. More than that, the owner has to be able to explain the formula that made the first shop a success to someone else.

In an ideal world the expansion issue should form part of the original location decision. If the owner is not seeking to multiply, the potential for building onto the initial premises is a key factor. Sometimes this can be a relatively simple matter, sometimes building another floor or a new bay can change the whole character of the business, a statement that leads neatly onto the issue of store design and layout.

Keypoint summary

1. Various analytical techniques are available to help with location decisions but their complexity and the availability and cost of data implies that the independent retailer may be poorly placed to use them.
2. The growth in shopping centres, particulary those out of town, points the way to the future for all retailers.
3. The growth in value of a retail property can be a significant element in the long-term benefit to the independent retailer.
4. Certain types of retailer can benefit from the creation and promotion of speciality centres.
5. Expansion by opening a second shop or building on to the first, involves fundamentally different issues for the retailer.

CHAPTER 5

Store Design and Layout

In 1610 Ben Johnson wrote a comedy entitled *The Alchemist*. In one scene Abel Drugger, a would-be tobacconist, enquires of the Alchemist as to how he should design his shop:

> I would know, by art, sir, of your worship which way I should make my door, by necromancie And, where my shelves And, which should be for boxes, And, which for pots.

Necromancie is another word for magic, and what is remarkable about the piece is that after over a quarter of a millenium we are still arguing about where to put doors and shelves and where to display what merchandise. There are nearly as many 'golden rules' as there are people breaking them and making money despite doing so. The only hard-and-fast rules are for the retailer to be analytical about what is being done, so that changes can be made to improve the business. To review the areas for decision and analysis, it is as well to start from the street and work inwards.

The name above the door

Even the largest of businesses trade under the names of their owners, past or present: Marks and Spencer, Laura Ashley, Sainsbury and

Selfridges. Others trade under names that were made up or evolved from some long forgotten company name, examples include Asda, Tesco, BHS and ELS. A third category were selected to add something to the shop with the idea that the name would symbolise the retail ethos of the company. Examples would include Bodyshop, Next, Top Man, Habitat, Safeway, KwikSave. Each name evokes something of the retailer itself.

Of the three types of name the last is probably the most preferable, followed by the proprieter's name with the more clinical names being the most difficult to relate to perhaps. The problem for the smaller business is to choose a name that is distinctive, compatible with the image to be presented to the customer and at the same time to choose one that no-one else has already registered as a trading name.

Store designers sometimes argue that the lettering of the name and certainly the colourways used in foreground and background are just as important but here we stray into the third area, of the symbolism of colour. First the outside look of the store itself.

The shop front

The shop front is the first introduction the customer has to the business. The retailer can ignore its potential and concentrate on other ways of enticing people through the door, or design a window that will both attract and sell what is on offer inside.

The first task is to attract attention. Practitioners argue the need for balance in window presentation.[1] Figure 5.1 illustrates two ways of achieving this using either a geometrically symmetric format or deliberately contrasting one side of a window with another while still attaining balance in the asymmetric format.

Within any display, colour contrast must be used sparingly, concentrating on using complementary colours or shades of the same colour. The colour wheel in Figure 5.2 identifies those adjacent colours that complement and those non-adjacent that contrast.

There should be some logic behind the grouping of products and supporting material in any display. If the juxtaposition of unassociated products is deliberately chosen to surprise, it must be obvious that surprise was intended, rather than that the products were thrown aimlessly together more in the hope than the expectation of creating an effect!

Window-dressing is an artistic activity and if retailers have neither the ability themselves or cannot afford to employ someone who has, then they are better not to add to the often appalling sights presented by the windows of independent stores and mask out their windows

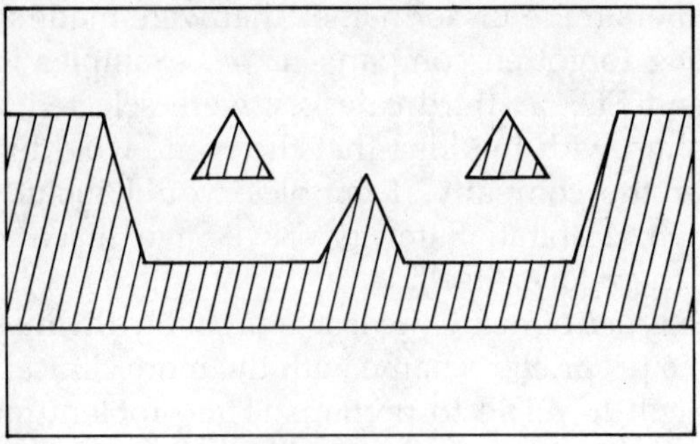

Symmetrical balance

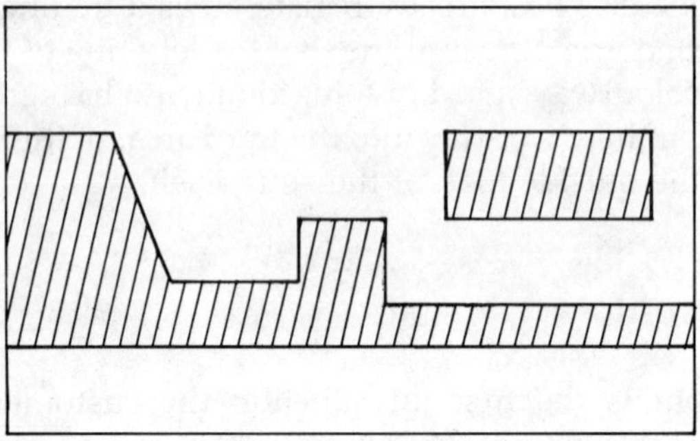

Asymmetrical balance

Figure 5.1 Achieving balance in a window display

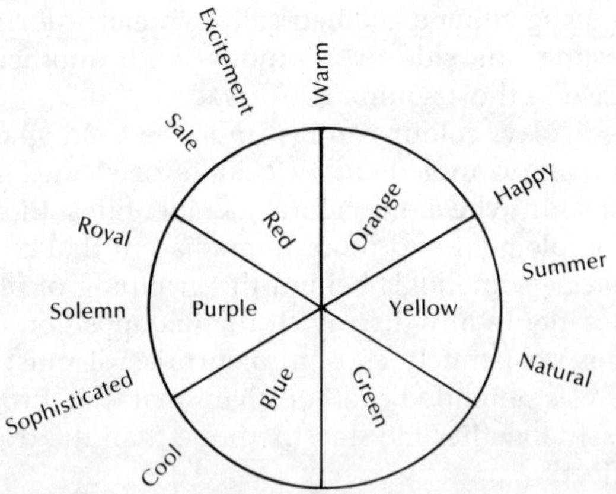

Figure 5.2 The colour wheel and symbolism

entirely. There is nothing quite so off-putting than the peeling paint and yellowed labels that pass for shop frontages and displays in many village shops. The impression of 'couldn't care less' is imparted, albeit subliminally, to the customer. Why do such retailers express surprise when their customers desert them in droves to the pristine new Sainsbury, even though it is a ten-minute bus ride away?

A traditional window display was expected to be fairly permanent. Perhaps because plate-glass was expensive or perhaps because the shop would be closed more hours than it was open, the temptation in the past was always to overcrowd the window display. Nowadays people have less time to inspect a window and more attractive and entertaining things to look at in their homes. Windows have become less crowded and tend to be redecorated more frequently. Traditionally-dressed windows often acted as barriers to entry because customers could not see into the shop.

The colour used for the shop frontage can also be a useful aid to projecting the character of the shop or even in making a statement about it. When the direct sales tour operator Tjaereborg first came to Britain, independent travel agents were concerned about their competitive position. One entrepreneurial agent used an identical shade of green to the distinctive colour of Tjaereborg's frontage to repaint his shop. The intention was to imply the same value for money offer of the discounter.

Travel agency represents one retail sector which seems to ignore the potential of window display outside of the summer season when last minute bargains are heavily promoted. The potential exists to carry a number of themes throughout the year, featuring the combined offers of different operators to the same market or novel ideas such as speciality weekend breaks. The shop frontage is an opportunity to begin selling to the customer that is often missed.

Store layout

Layout depends very much upon the size of the shop and the products or services being sold, but some principles apply whatever the business. The most important is maximising the opportunity for the customer to be exposed to what is on offer.

Counter-service shops, where all the merchandise is held behind the server, might give the image of being quaint and they might suffer less pilferage than a self-service store, but it is difficult to see how such a format maximises sales. Customers have to ask for everything and must queue longer to be served unless the retailer spends more on staffing.

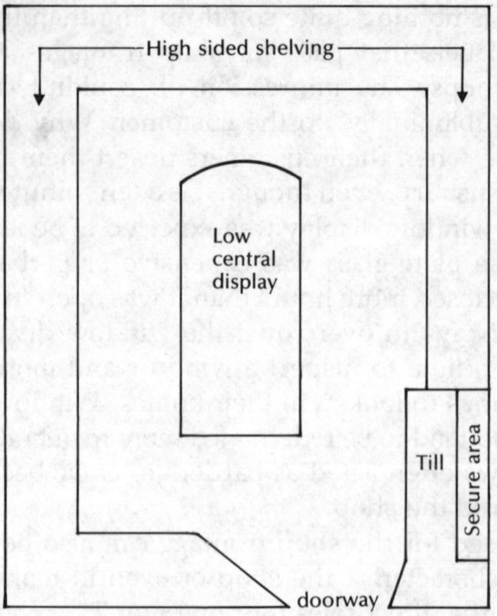

Figure 5.3 Floor plan for a small self-service grocery/convenience store

Figures 5.3 and 5.4 present two plans for the layout of a small grocers and an estate agency. Neither relies upon counter-service. The layout for the grocers will not appear particularly novel. The estate agency plan by contrast moves away from using the walls as the main method of display and uses multisided, vertical displays scattered in the centre of the shop. Gone is the often forbidding counter and instead two desks, emphasising informality. The small office is retained for more confidential exchanges.

Figure 5.3 uses the idea of imposing a circulation on the customer flow. It is difficult to pick up just one item and go straight to the till. Cigarettes and spirits could well be held next to the till for ease of security and because cigarettes are one of a few purchases that are normally made singly.

The floor plan assumes a clockwise flow. Some claim that this is the preferred way for people to circulate, implying a right-hand doorway and till.[2] Others dismiss the idea.[3] What is important is to try and establish a flow pattern. One exception to this rule is the estate agent layout where an attempt has been made to make people browse rather than have them enter the shop, ask for printed details and leave quickly.

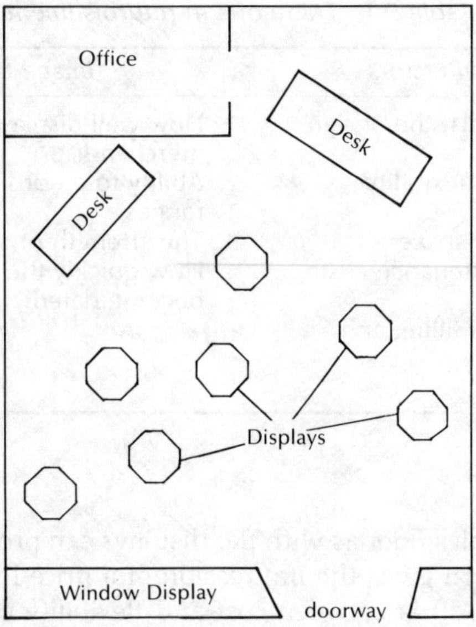

Figure 5.4 Floor plan for an estate agency

Trade-offs in store design

Furbishment costs in retailing can be prohibitively high for the smaller business. Figures of £40 per square foot were not uncommon in the 1980s. The large multiple can afford to experiment, to convert one or two shops and measure the effect on trade. The smaller business has no such opportunity for experimentation and may choose to design and even construct fitments themselves.

There are a number of trade-offs inherent in store design. The major ones are between strictly financial factors, the main one being the purchase cost of the fixturing, and the image factors refurbishment seeks to enhance.[4] Table 5.1 illustrates the kind of factors that have to be traded off.

Many of the factors are self-explanatory, one or two might benefit from greater explanation. For example, labour costs in maintaining a good display can be a crucial factor. Wages can account for up to a third of all costs. Staff should not have to spend their time tidying merchandise because it becomes untidy quickly. A system of hanging garments rather than placing them flat can be far more labour efficient, encourage people to touch the merchandise but be less efficient in terms of stock density. Attempts to achieve the same stock

Table 5.1 Trade-offs in refurbishment

Financial factors	*Image factors*
1. Cost of materials, the design itself	1. How well displayed is the merchandise
2. Durability and flexibility	2. Ability to co-ordinate allied ranges
3. Efficient use of space	3. The strength of any symbolism
4. Cleaning, maintenance costs	4. How quickly the concept will become dated
5. Labour costs in filling and maintaining	
6. Security	

density on the sales floor as with flat displays can produce a crowded look which in turn gives the impression of a price-led operation.

A major trade-off is between cost and flexibility on the one hand and symbolism and how long a design concept will last on the other. Ralph Halpern of the Burton group claimed in the 1980s that a fashion design concept had a life of as little as three to five years, for example.

In the late 1980s a number of menswear retailers were moving towards what became known as a 'clubby' image.[5] Some went for darker woods such as mahogany and cherry. Leather chairs were a favourite feature. Shop windows reverted to the styles of an earlier era. The problem here is that the look was so distinctive that the fitments would be difficult to use in five or ten year's time if the idea became dated.

How should the smaller business select?

Investment in furbishments is one of the more crucial decisions a retailer has to make as the store design is probably the main method of creating and projecting an image. It follows that the main criterion must be the ability of the design concept to deliver the chosen image, an image which must be differentiated from the images projected by competition.

Because the smaller business cannot experiment as much as its multiple rivals, the financial decision must be based more on the judgement of the owner than rational measurement of likely increases in traffic flow. Flexibility would appear to be far more important, allowing some opportunity for change if the idea does not work as well as expected. It would also be worthwhile calculating the increase in trade or margin that would be needed to support any planned refurbishment.

In practice the independent retailer seems to rely more upon a 'do it yourself' philosophy to reduce costs. The design of one menswear outlet in Wilmslow, south Manchester, was the creation of its owner.[6] The atmosphere was very much the clubby concept referred to earlier, but the planning and building of fitments had been mainly the work of the owner, who spent a great deal of time touring the country looking for new ideas.

Other ambiance factors

Ambiance includes many intangible factors and also others such as heat, light, sound and smell. Laymen refer to six senses, psychologists claim we may have as many as 20. Whatever the truth, customers absorb information about a store through more than just their eyes.

Energy costs and their control became major issues in retailing in the 1970s following two major rises in the price of crude oil. By the middle 1980s inflation, the inability of OPEC to manipulate oil prices, and a glut of the commodity that dominates world trade, had reduced the percentage of total costs due to heat and light. Some shops, even small shops, began to install air-conditioning instead of ventilation systems (or no systems at all) to improve the ambiance for customers and staff.

The value of background music is a topic that creates a good deal of debate. Purchases such as furniture, cars, holidays and houses represent substantial decisions. Many of us would rather avoid making a decision at all, than risk making a bad one. We get flustered and start looking for the door. Background music chosen for the relaxing mood it evokes could be useful in helping those of us who might leave rather than make a decision. By the way of contrast, the latest pop music could be useful background in the shop selling teenage fashion, especially casual wear.

Hygiene is a vital factor in food retailing. A hygienic image involves not only a clean environment, but also good practice by staff. Handling food with bare hands, counter staff blowing noses or even coughing over exposed food, dirty overalls and unclean fingernails are all factors that could impact upon the hygiene standards of the store. More important, customers' perceptions will be that the store is unhygienic.

Smell is linked to hygiene in food retailing. A shop selling wet fish has to be careful to vent the area directly to the outside of the store to avoid the negative effects of a fishy odour throughout the shop. However, an instore bakery can be vented into the store or onto the street above the shop entrance. The smell of fresh baked bread is a positive rather than negative feature.

Smell also seems to be important in clothing retailing. Changing rooms must smell nice or at least not musty. A menswear retailer can even benefit from a slight background odour of leather and polish.[7]

Keypoint summary

1. Store design and layout are key factors in retailing by projecting the desired image and improving the shopping environment.
2. Individual factors have to be traded-off in selecting a shop design, in particular display and labour cost. The smaller business is well advised to select a flexible solution.
3. A store's ambiance can be determined by interior design but other factors such as noise and smell can be important.

CHAPTER 6

Merchandising

The topics of store design and product merchandising are closely related. A good layout, effective lighting and appropriate fixturing can change the perception shoppers have of a product. However, once the retailer has decided on a store layout, the emphasis shifts to decisions on what products go where and on minor changes in product display.

Decisions such as these used to be the sole responsibility of the store manager irrespective of the size of the business. Most multiples have now centralised their decision-making on both product selection and product merchandising.[1] Some multiples operate a number of formats allowing them flexibility to cater for stores of different sizes and local trading conditions. Centralised decision-making on stocking and display focuses on the profitability of individual product lines. The concept is simple enough, each product is charged a notional 'rent' for occupying a shelf or a display. The more the product sells and the higher the margin, the more space it can occupy. It can also be allocated to a better space.

The same philosophy should be used by the smaller retailer. Unfortunately many owners/managers do not have the data necessary to identify even which lines are selling well, let alone which are making most profit for them. They have a feel for what is selling naturally enough but either do not tend to have the time or make the time to be more analytical about space allocation. The purpose of this chapter is therefore to assess a number of ideas that could be used by many smaller retailers of products in improving profitability by improving merchandising.

What is a good position?

The previous chapter introduced the need to impose a logical flow around most shops. This implies a certain order for products. A common piece of advice is to place high service lines towards the back of a store and browsing lines towards the front. The idea being that people are drawn through the displays and buy more than they planned to. In one study nearly two-thirds of items purchased in shopping trips to supermarkets were unplanned purchases.[2] It follows that it is important to encourage people to examine as high a percentage of stock as possible.

Certain places in any store are regarded as good selling positions because they seem to attract people's attention. These include eye-level on shelving, the aisle ends on any display system and the second row back on a counter-top merchandiser next to a till. Again the standard advice is to use such locations for faster-selling lines to maximise their rate of sale,[3] although the advice varies with one source recommending aisle ends for discounting or end-of-line sales.[4] Only experience will determine what goes best and where, the only rule appears to be that 'hot spots' as they are called will exist in any store. It follows that they should be identified.

Horizontal and vertical blocking

Most large retailers merchandise similar products in one vertical block display. This aids selection as the customer can stand in front of one section of shelving to make a choice. Many smaller retailers use horizontal blocking, carrying similar products along a shelf. One writer argues in favour of his approach in the context of independent retailing, explaining that the approach matches the way the human eye travels.[5] The same explanation is used by another author to recommend vertical blocking.[6]

It may well be that horizontal blocking in a smaller shop has its advantages. One retailer used the approach in his convenience store because it encouraged someone who had come in for a single item, a packet of cereal for example, to walk along the shelving. In this way the shopper would be exposed to other products and be more likely to make a second purchase.

The larger the shop, and more it is used for a complete shopping expedition, the less effective horizontal blocking is likely to be, as it would serve to irritate the regular shopper and confuse the person seeking just one item.

Display techniques

Discussions on vertical and horizontal blocking are more relevant to retailers of packeted products or of fashion separates. Retailers of housewares, textiles and many fashion items will employ in-store displays for customers to browse through. The rules of display (if they exist at all) change. Regimentation is undesirable, an interesting and stimulating presentation is all important.

Four different types of display arrangement have been identified.[7] These are represented in Figure 6.1. No one method has anything in particular to commend it although the pyramid approach is recommended for displays of products of mixed size and the fan approach as the basis for fashion displays. It follows that any fitments purchased should be as flexible as possible to allow the retailer to change a display arrangement periodically.

Certain products require specialist display methods because of the nature of the product. The list is a long one, from frozen products to

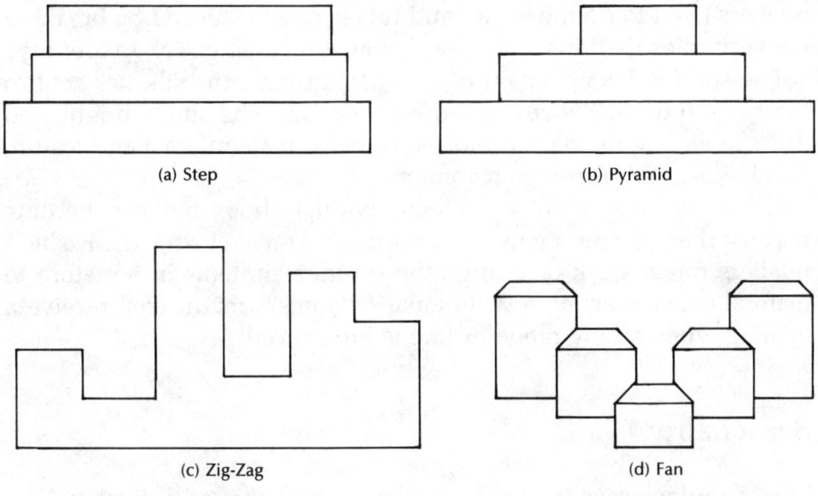

Figure 6.1 Four types of display arrangement

hi-fi, but a few examples will serve as a reminder that generalisations about display techniques in retailing are not always useful to the practitioner.

Jewellery, for example, because of its size value, needs special care in its presentation. A number of display techniques have been used by various retailers, largely aimed at reducing barriers between staff, products and customers, but with all such experiments being limited by the need for security. Most display techniques use variants on a similar theme of a shadow box, a small display case with a high level of illumination. Such are the margins on jewellery and such are the unit prices that display densities can be very low. Those jewellery retailers who have managed to differentiate themselves on image have chosen to modify the often standardised display methods in this sector. The emphasis here is not then on identifying good positions in store or on standard display formats but rather on innovation in display technique.

Creating interest

The danger of trying to identify rules in merchandising technique is that one will break the only real rule that exists in displaying goods, that is, the need to stimulate customers into buying because they find themselves attracted to merchandise. Writers on retailing talk about bringing theatre into the store.[8] Even the Royal Shakespeare Company will try to introduce something new, something startling into its next production of one of the bard's plays. The point is that retailers need to do the same, and this is often achieved by breaking the very rules that this and other books on retailing seek to identify.

The sudden juxtaposition of the incongruous; the silk ties sold in the book shop in the run up to Fathers' Day; the single bright, red dress in among the pastel colours; all help create interest and lead to purchases and returning customers.

Customers are often loyal to individual shops but can become bored if there is nothing new to tempt them on a return visit. Fashion retailers rotate stock or change the position of items in the store to maintain customer interest. Regular customers might well receive a mailing when a new range or line is introduced.

Seasonality

The changing seasons offer a good reason to change a display. Few products are without a seasonality in their sales. Retail sales nationally peak in the final quarter of the year.[9] The difference in sales of slippers, swimwear and suntan cream will be expected, but other products such as Cola will peak twice a year in summer and at Christmas. Toys peak heavily at Christmas, perfume follows suit but sales rocket again prior to Mother's Day.

Other similar trends are less apparent but are just as predictable. There has been an economic boom prior to almost every General Election since the war. Blatant tax reductions have now been replaced by fortuitous changes in interest rates as their cause. People will tend to buy more and also more expensive items at such times.

Relying on the manufacturer

Manufacturer's representatives are keen to convince the retailer that the retailer would benefit by giving certain products better display. Confectionery companies such as Mars offer companies merchandising plans for a wide range of products, including those of their competitors, with the promise to maximise the retailer's total sales of sweets.

Many companies produce merchandising units and fixtures ranging from self-servers to garment racks. The problem facing the shopkeeper is that it is difficult to be sure whether the retailer's interests are being considered. It is not unknown for a retailer to find a representative busily constructing a display on the premises without permission! Nevertheless, some manufacturers have invested heavily in researching methods of displaying their products that maximise sales in a given physical area. Quite often these merchandising solutions increase the stock density on a given floor space, improve display and produce higher sales per square foot that benefit both supplier and retailer.

Some manufacturers work closely with retailers to maximise sales of the manufacturer's lines. Unless the manufacturer is also a small company, the small retailer will be unlikely to receive the same help. Nabisco offered a computerised space-planning system in the 1980s, Spaceman, that produces a simulation of a run of shelving as one of its outputs. Knowledge of the market share for each product allows the system to optimise the shelf space and position for each product. At the time of writing it was hoped to extend the service to the smaller retailer.

Space and shelf allocation

As implied at the beginning of this chapter, it should be possible for any retailer to be more analytical about space and shelf allocation. The

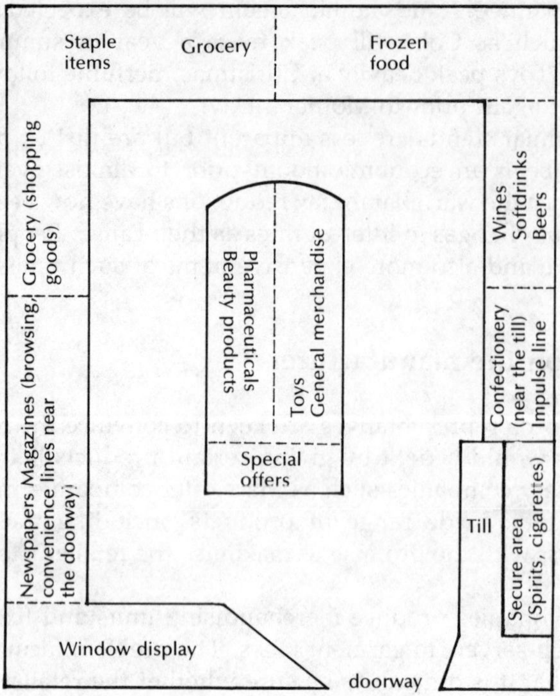

Figure 6.2 Space allocation in a convenience store

first task is to divide the shop-floor area up into zones and allocate each merchandise category its appropriate space. This decision is based upon the profitability of the product category to the retailer and the need to create the customer flow discussed earlier. Figure 6.2 illustrates the kind of decisions that could be made. The floor plan is that from Figure 5.3.

The suggested layout places the staple items such as bread, milk, frozen peas and butter towards the back of the shop, encouraging people round all the other merchandise. Browsing lines have been placed near the doorway to make people stop. Some newspapers and magazines will be regarded as convenience products too. Special offers are given prominence at the aisle end to encourage extra purchases and create interest. Slower selling but higher margin lines, aspirin, vitamin tablets, hairspray, are placed where the offtake is expected to be slowest. Frozen food comes at the end of the grocery section so that the shopper can put such lines on the top of the bag. Products with a greater risk of being stolen are kept behind the till, but other alcoholic drink is on open display. Lines appealing to

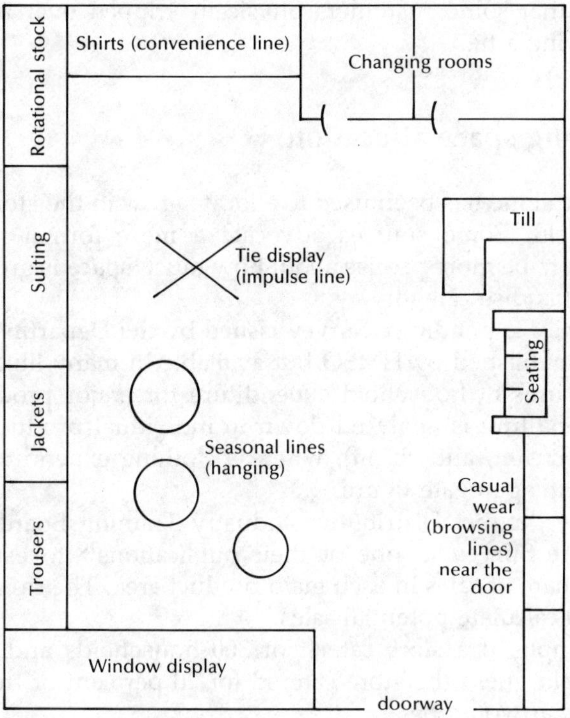

Figure 6.3 Space allocation in a menswear outlet

children come nearer to the till, such as confectionery and small toys, partly for security, partly for the impulse nature of the purchase by adults.

Figure 6.3 shows a possible layout for a menswear retailer. Plainer shirts, suitable for work, are placed to the rear of the shop – the highest routine purchase item at the back of the store. Casual wear including jumpers and casual shirts are near the door. Being a high-service retailer by comparison with the convenience store, there is a need to stop the customer until an assistant is available. A good deal of potential selling space is also taken up by seating for anyone with the customer and also by changing rooms. The main product offer, suits, jackets and trousers are away from the door. Either an assistant leads the customer here or they arrive having already been exposed to the display near the doorway and the seasonal lines in the centre floor display.

Ties are an impulse line for many men who may buy one to go with a suit or jacket. Putting them in the middle of the floor is an example of using surprise. The manager of the shop this idea came from explained that some customers physically tripped over the display before buying a tie.

Calculating space allocation

So far logic alone has been used to allocate areas in the store for each product field. Some sources advocate a more formal method of calculation to be more precise about how much space is given over to each merchandise category.

The Family Expenditure Survey issued by the Department of Employment published by HMSO but available in many libraries, contains measures of household expenditure for major product areas. Food expenditure is analysed down to individual products (butter, sugar, ice cream, and so on), whereas clothing expenditure is presented as an aggregate figure.

The now defunct Distributive Industry Training Board used the Expenditure Survey in one of their publications[10] to estimate the retailers' share of sales in each main product area. The same idea can be used to calculate potential sales.

For example, if a store caters for 300 households and the shopkeeper could guess the store catered for 20 per cent of their needs, sales of sugar would be

$$\text{Weekly household expenditure on sugar} \times 300 \times \frac{20}{100}$$

= (using 1986 figures) £18.60 per week[11]

This would represent sales of about 372-kilo bags of sugar each week. A similar calculation on tea would yield 130 $\frac{1}{4}$lb packets of tea each week.

Unfortunately, a bag of sugar takes more space than a packet of tea but, if the shopowner has the time to make the same calculation for each product type, the relative importance of each can be estimated and more facings and better facings allocated to the potentially higher-volume lines.

Product depth and width

Because smaller retailers tend to be less analytical about their businesses, some decisions tend to be neglected . One of the more apparent problems lies in too wide a range of similar products being carried within a product type. Sometimes too broad a choice is offered, low fat spread, low cholesterol margarine, margarine and butter blends, traditional margarine and each in three sizes. Too wide a range of similar products is a more prevalent problem than too deep a range of associated products. This may be due to wanting to offer choice as mentioned in chapter 2, or because of the persuasive qualities of manufacturers' representatives. In one survey by one of the authors the average number of brands of washing-up liquid carried by major multiples was just over three. One small shop, with far less space than in the typical multiple, carried no fewer than nine brands.

Table 6.1 shows how a retailer can make decisions on the width and depth of a range and the space allocated to each line. For the sake of illustration all lines are assumed to be of comparable physical size, that is, they can all fit similar shelving. In part of a store there are four product types, (1), (2), (3) and (4). Within each product type there are a number of brands or different sizes of the same brand. Selling prices vary, as do gross margins.

By knowing the selling price, gross margin and number of units sold the gross profit per week can be calculated. By knowing the percentage of space each product line occupies the true contribution to the business can be estimated by the gross profit divided by the relative space the line is allocated.

The area yields £47.34 gross profit in total. Six product lines, D, E, I, K, P and Q out of the 17 account for £32.73 or nearly 70 per cent of this total. Many businesses find similar ratios, the minority of products contributing the majority of profit.

Product type (1) occupies 15 per cent of space but yields only £3.14 gross profit, an average profit to space ratio of 0.2 or less than half the average of 0.47. Variant C can be deleted freeing up space. It may be possible to reduce the space allocated to type (1) products still further. To achieve the average ratio, type (1) should be allocated 6 per cent of space. Whether such a move is totally desirable is a matter for judgement. The product might be eliminated or perhaps it is already on a low shelf where it might be expected to sell less well.

Almost the opposite action is called for in type (2) products. They occupy 13 per cent of space and yield nearly 37 per cent of profit. The space allocated could be doubled and there is the potential to introduce other variants to widen or deepen the range.

Product type (3) offers the greatest challenge. The range contains only three lines, L, M and N that are clearly struggling but none is doing outstandingly well. Margins on L and M are low and could be raised, although deleting M and N would seem to be the best action and using the space to introduce a new product area entirely or expand type (2) products.

Type (4) products present a good example of how space allocation and profitability must not be the sole consideration in retailing.

Table 6.1 Product width and depth space allocation

Line	*Product type*	*Selling price*	*Gross margin (%)*	*No. sold per wk*	*Gross profit (£/wk)*	*% Space*	*Gross profit/ % space*	*Action on line*	*Action on range*
A	(1)	0.35	20	20	1.40	5	0.28	Retain	
B	(1)	0.36	15	30	1.62	5	0.32	Retain	Reduce space
C	(1)	0.40	15	2	0.12	5	0.02	Delete	
D	(2)	0.90	15	40	5.40	4	1.35	Retain & expand	
E	(2)	0.92	15	60	8.28	3	2.76	Retain & expand	Increase space and range
F	(2)	0.80	20	10	1.60	3	0.53	Retain	
G	(2)	0.70	20	15	2.10	3	0.70	Retain	
H	(3)	1.70	15	10	2.55	5	0.51	Retain	
I	(3)	1.80	15	15	4.05	5	0.81	Retain	
J	(3)	2.00	10	8	1.60	5	0.32	Retain but increase margin	
K	(3)	2.00	20	10	4.00	6	0.67	Retain	Reduce space by deleting M and N
L	(3)	1.80	10	5	0.90	6	0.15	Retain and increase margin	
M	(3)	1.60	10	2	0.32	6	0.05	Delete	
N	(3)	1.60	15	2	0.48	5	0.10	Delete	
O	(3)	1.60	20	6	1.92	4	0.48	Retain	
P	(4)	0.50	20	50	5.00	15	0.33	Retain	Consider increasing selling price
Q	(4)	0.50	20	60	6.00	15	0.40	Retain	
				Total	47.34	100	0.47(Av.)		

Although the products contribute at slightly below average levels and occupy a good deal of space, they sell in large numbers. These may well be the traffic builders in the store. There may be a case for reducing their space allocation to 20 or 25 per cent of space, to bring the contribution more in line with the average, but equally there may be a case for retaining the space allocation, and increasing the selling price. Again only the owner's judgement can have the final word.

The principles of space allocation in proportion to profitability, while retaining a logical flow around the store, are the same for any product retailer. Another example is contained in the Health Food Retailer case study (Case Study B). Defining what to select as space to be allocated can be more difficult in some sectors than in others. A furniture and furnishings retailer might use both floor and walls to present merchandise and see little sense in allocating the same costs to both. The same retailer might also have problems allocating floor space between items in the same way as a grocer allocates shelf space. Similarly a butcher might ponder on the value of space allocation when his display is just a window area. However, both need to consider whether their more profitable lines are being displayed in the best part of the shop. The furniture retailer might be surprised as to how profitable are the pictures and grandmother clocks that are stocked more as peripheral items to tables and chairs. The butcher may also like to consider the potential of using more counter space as chilled areas to present a wider choice of cuts or even to experiment with the space allocated to different products in the window display.

Keypoint summary

1. There are good and not so good selling sites in any store, although opinions sometimes vary on where they are and which products to feature there. To identify them a retailer needs good sales information.
2. There are few reliable rules in display other than the need for logic, to stimulate the shopper and to be aware of factors such as seasonality. A manufacturer's display can be a good option for the smaller business.
3. Space allocation must be done systematically (but rarely is so) by allocating each product and product type space proportional to its profitability.

CHAPTER 7

Pricing and Promotion

While the independent retailer has to avoid or minimise price competition, price levels form a central component of any retail business. Since Retail Price Maintenance (RPM) was removed in 1964, retailers have been free to charge whatever price they wished for all goods other than books, newspapers, magazines and some pharmaceuticals. That said, there have been instances of manufacturers denying supplies to retailers who they feel have cut selling prices of specific brands too far.

Even if the independent retailer can avoid most of the problems of price competition, goods still have to be priced. The basic methods of pricing for the business to make an overall profit are covered in this chapter. The purpose of the first half of this chapter is to examine how smaller retailers can manage the issue of price once the overall pricing method has been set.

Competition

The typical small retailer will compete with businesses of similar size and with the multiples. Some knowledge of where a business stands with respect to competition is essential. Most business people have a feel for where they are in the price spectrum, but surveys of salespeople, for instance, have indicated that most feel they sell at above average price. In other words, salespeople believe they have a price problem. It is likely that this extends to small retailers who lack the market research data available to the multiples on price comparisons. Greville Havenhand in *Nation of Shopkeepers*[1] recalls the reluctance of staff in a London grocers to increase prices by 10 per cent despite the poor financial state of the business. The employee's opinion was that such an increase would make them totally uncompetitive, until one of them was sent to purchase a basket of items in a competitor's shop to discover the competitor's selling prices were exactly 10 per cent higher than their own.

Keeping a check on the selling price of at least the major items in competitive stores is essential to all retailers.

Known value items

If retailers are sometimes in the dark about their relative selling prices, so are their customers. However, some customers will spend a deal of time comparison shopping. The usual behaviour pattern is not to assess prices for all items but against a number of key items, sometimes referred to as Known Value Items (KVIs). Often these are leading brands such as Heinz Beans, or Fairy Liquid, or a standard commodity such as a loaf of bread, a pair of tights or a gallon of petrol. A retailer can give the impression of being price competitive by holding margins and prices down on at least a selection of KVIs.

The grocery retailer is somewhat more exposed in pricing terms because shoppers will also cost the total price of a 'shopping basket'. Most households consume a predictable range of products each week. These are replaced regularly in the weekly shop. The purchaser will be sensitive to the total price paid for their regular basket. Larger retailers are well aware of the typical basket bought by their target customers and adjust their selling prices accordingly. It is here that the smaller retailer with higher relative overheads and lower purchasing power cannot hope to compete just on price.

Standard mark-up versus market pricing

The normal method of pricing in retail is to mark up the purchase price by a standard percentage, rounding off the resultant calculation. The mark-up varies by product type and can often vary considerably within a single small shop. Some products such as jewellery and greetings cards will stand margins of up to 100 per cent, while margins on cigarettes and tobacco are often below 10 per cent.[2]

The problem with this essentially cost plus approach is that it can ignore the reality of what the market will bear. Prices for similar items carried by local competition offer both a guide to market conditions and a constraint on the maximum price that can be set. A novel product, however, can be hopelessly underpriced, particularly if the retailer uses margins obtainable on standard lines as a guide. Too low a price for such an item might even restrict sales as customers are used to paying for novelty.

Manufacturers' price lists

While the ending of RPM made it illegal for manufacturers to impose a selling price, their suggested prices are still the main reference point for retailers. Independent guides, such as Shaws, carry price lists and most wholesalers carry manufacturers' lists. The manufacturer's price could not be referred to at the time of writing as a reference point in discounting or operating a sale under the Price Marking (Bargain Offers) Orders.

Multiple retailers have employed the device of double pricing, offering goods in one store at one price and subsequently announcing a sale in the rest of the chain at a lower price. It is likely that this potential loophole in legislation will be closed, but the example is another one that works in favour of the multiple.

Simplifying price points

If a retailer carries 1000 lines, then having 1000 different prices should be avoided. Some products fall naturally into narrow price bands. Some product fields extend across wide price ranges. There are two reasons why retailers should aim to simplify their price points and try to operate using a limited number of prices.

The first advantage is to make it easier for employees in pricing up goods and cashing up purchases. A similar advantage accrues to the buyer who can be set fixed selling points for merchandise. American fashion retailers have a labelling system for pricing points couched in terms indicating merchandise quality; economy; moderate; better; best. For a given merchandise type, price points can be set to guide buyers in selecting merchandise.

Finally price lining, as it is sometimes called, can aid customer selection in fashion goods. Rather than have to select from merchandise priced at many separate price points, it is often better to price line to say three price points. The customer selects the relevant price point and then one item from the range. While too simplified a system may give the impression of limited choice, the advantages of simplification in managing a business of any size cannot be underestimated.

Ticketing

Opinions vary yet again on the best approach to presenting the price on the product. The practice generally has changed from using bold ticketing to smaller type faces but including more information for the customer on the ticket. The shopkeeper, too, can benefit from including more data on the price ticket. Systems such as Kimball tags allow reordering from collected sales tags. One writer advises including the retailer's purchase price, in code, on the tag to aid in the calculation of gross profit[3] on an on-going basis.

After the merchandise itself, the price ticket is the thing that customers examine most closely. The smaller shop can do itself a deal of harm with poorly-presented ticketing, and help its image by clear well-presented tickets with possibly some extra information for the customer about the product.

Most retailers include Value Added Tax in their selling prices. Some, such as builders merchants, who also sell to tradespeople do not. One small shop who catered more for the DIY trade than the professional always priced exclusive of VAT, arguing perhaps that the prices looked lower as a result. This caused some resentment among customers who nicknamed the owner 'and yer VAT' after what became his trade mark when announcing the bill. The reader may well point out that this at least made the retailer distinctive. It did, but not in a positive way. When a competitor opened nearby who displayed inclusive prices, customers could indeed differentiate between the two shops and went to the new one instead.

Sales promotions

If price is a dangerous area for the independent retailer to use as a strategy, it can still be used as a tactic to good effect. Price promotion can have a number of objectives:

1. Increase customer flow into the shop.
2. Persuade customers to benefit from a special offer and buy something unplanned.
3. Encourage multiple purchase.
4. Improve image and thus patronage.
5. Clear slow-selling, unseasonal or end-of-line items.

Each objective, other than perhaps the fourth, is tactical, short term rather than long term. Prices are cut on selected lines for a limited period only. Price levels on KVIs may be held lower for longer to give the impression of price competitiveness.

Advertising

Advertising expenditure by the retail sector has been rising faster in real terms than in allied sectors, and in particular manufacturing. In some sections of the retail trade, manufacturer advertising is considerably less than retailer advertising.

A major theme in this book is the differentiation of the retail store from its competition, the creation of an identifiable and hopefully unique offer that allows the retailer to avoid mere price competition. Manufacturers have solved what appears to be a similar problem in differentiating their products and marketing brands rather than commodity items. A key to a successful brand is acknowledged to be advertising. Few brands, if any, have become established and have succeeded in the long term without heavyweight consumer advertising aimed at creating a favourable image for the brand.

It seems logical that retailers seeking a differentiated image should look to advertising to help create that image. Many multiple retailers have tried to change their image by advertising. But other multiples have chosen not to advertise. As these retailers also have a clear image in the market-place, as was argued in chapter 3 and elsewhere, advertising may not be helpful in image creation.[4]

In a review of the role of retailer advertising, Christina Fulop[5] concluded that retailers used advertising more to inform than create image. They tend to use press advertising rather than television, while brand manufacturers use more television than print, using the more appropriate medium for image creation.

Another writer, Eric Lowe,[6] claims that good (retail) advertising sells both the goods *and* the store, but points out that what must be avoided is selling a position in the market-place, that is, an image, that the public do not accept. Lowe sees two roles for retailer advertising in the management of image, first – to develop the business within its existing position in the market-place and second – to reflect the true image of the store.

It follows that something else helps create the image in the first place. In a series of studies on image management[7] in the multiple sector, one of the authors concluded that the key determinants of retail image were, in order of effect:

Store design
Store personnel (especially service given)
Merchandise (range and price levels)

The role of advertising in image was seen as informing customers and potential customers about a store's image, not in creating it.

Low cost advertising

The smaller business cannot consider the potential for large-scale advertising, basically because the amount that will be spent for each potential customer is too high. Even the cheapest packages marketed by television companies will be too expensive when measured by the cost per customer approach.

The independent retailer is likely to use the services of highly-localised media, free sheets and other local papers and posters, handbills, direct mail and possibly cinema and radio advertising. One independent grocer, for example, chose leaflets. 3000 cost £3000 in 1987 to produce and deliver, but sales doubled as a result.[8] Some retailers may be able to justify television if, as in the case of car retailers, there is manufacturer support or the catchment area for the business is large. There will be exceptions. For the majority the promotional budget will be low.

If advertising is an ineffective way of creating a favourable image for a shop, then large expenditures are going to be difficult to justify. That said, it is easy to forget the other, informative role of retailer advertising. Customers cannot be expected to be aware of every aspect of a retailer's business. Some purchases are made infrequently. Furniture purchasing, for example, is associated with certain events such as moving house or marriage. On average, households buy furniture only once every six months. A specialist furniture retailer must therefore keep the market-place informed of its presence. Wedding dresses may be bought only once in a lifetime, and the occasional advertisement in a local paper and in Yellow Pages could be essential for the specialist shop catering for this market.

In 1988 the British government were planning to open local authority leisure centres up to commercial competition by allowing outside bids to manage such centres. One of the authors had worked sometime earlier with a local authority on the marketing of its leisure centres with one of the objectives being to minimise the financial deficit being incurred. One recommendation to the local authority was for a series of essentially low-cost promotional methods. In essence, the main promotional problem lay in the low expenditure typically incurred when visiting a leisure centre of between one and two pounds in 1985. Any promotion could not afford to cost more than about a pound for each extra visitor. Promotion at the time was limited to advertising in local newspapers and making leaflets available in the reception area at each centre.

Two of the ideas recommended for low-cost promotion were adopted. One was for display boards near each centre carrying simple announcements such as 'Play Squash Today' or 'Special Rates for Players who Swim'. Another was for greater involvement with the local media to encourage articles on leisure activities linked to individual centres. The full story is covered in one of the later case studies (Case Study C).

Special events

Special events fall more under the heading of public relations than advertising, but tend to be more under the control of the retailer. They range from authors signing books in a store to the tradition of Father Christmas. Fashion and department stores seem to be more involved in events than other types of retailing, with American stores being particularly inventive. One store in Atlanta invited in families with young children during a rebuilding programme. Each child was given a hard hat and 'helped' workmen build walls, mix mortar and move bricks. The same store offered Saturday courses on fashion and grooming for older children.

Direct mail

The example of the use of leafleting was given earlier for a grocery retailer. Targeted mailshots offer the retailer a potentially highly-cost-effective means of promotion. Retailers often gather the names and addresses of customers, on invoices and on delivery notes, for example. The information can be used to produce a mailing list of customers. If the post codes are available other potential customers can be targeted who live in the same road and who could well share the same life-style.

The staff of one fashion retailer kept detailed records on the purchases and attitudes of individual customers. Typical records contained notes such as 'interested in X designer clothes, 'phone when new range comes in' and 'buys only when with husband'. Sales assistants telephoned and wrote to customers tailoring their messages to the profile they maintained on each.

Staff incentives

Most promotions are aimed at the customer. Some can be better aimed at sales assistants. Some retailers give commission on sales. The disadvantages include the almost predatory attitude of assistants in fashion shops who rarely advise Madam that something does not suit her!

Manufacturers occasionally offer incentives for good sales performance by retail employees. Car salespeople will have incentives provided by the manufacturer. Fashion manufacturers might publish league tables of sales in each outlet carrying their lines which might again be linked to a reward system. Salespeople working for some American realtors (estate agents) might receive little or no basic salary and depend upon commission.

Few retailers of any size appear to profit share or offer staff bonus schemes linked directly to personal performance. The smaller the business, the less likely staff incentives seem to occur, somewhat surprising perhaps as the owners are, in practice, most certainly on an incentive scheme themselves.

Public relations

One area worthy of consideration for a local retailer is public relations. Serving the community means being involved with that community and being known within it. Public relations is not limited to sending an article to the local newspaper or negotiating editorial coverage in exchange for advertising. A school outfitters might offer a prize at the local school, a restaurant might sponsor a competition at the local sports centre, a garden centre a prize for the best-kept garden.

The idea is to find an idea that is associated with or complementary to the retailer's business. Requests for sponsorship of worthy causes are unlikely to be cost effective public relations and must be considered against other criteria. The retailer must have a clear policy and even a defined budget for public relations as much as advertising.

Defining promotional needs

A later chapter appraises the methods available to the smaller retailer in controlling the business, one principle being the definition of clear goals. It is worth examining promotional goals in the context of this chapter as the promotional goals for the independent retailer are likely to be easy to define.

One reason why Marks and Spencer chose not to advertise until 1988 was that their problem was not too few customers but too little merchandise to sell. A straightforward way of setting goals for retail promotion is in terms of customer flow. Once in the shop the reality of the offer is more important in determining the rate of sale of merchandise. It follows that promotional goals should be set in terms of the number of customers entering the store. To appraise the success or otherwise of promotion the retailer needs to know its customer flow rate and needs to measure any increase due to the promotion. Thereafter it is a simple matter to assess, by knowing the typical amount spent each customer visit and the average net margin, whether the promotion was cost effective.

Two guidelines on advertising seem relevant at this point. The first is the old addage that only half of advertising expenditure works, but no-one knows which half. The second is that there is a threshold of awareness that has to be breached before people notice advertising, unless they are looking for what is being promoted. Both guidelines mean that one advertisement or one promotional activity is unlikely to be effective on its own. Perhaps it was a bad idea, perhaps no-one saw the advertisement or read the leaflet because something else attracted their attention. Whatever the cause of any one failure, having that failure does not mean that advertising will not work for the business concerned.

In summary, a retailer needs first to define the objective for a promotion, probably in terms of customer flow. Secondly, the outcome should be measured, but the results of one attempt should not be taken as absolutely valid one way or another given the unpredictability of promotion.

Keypoint summary

1. The simple approach of cost plus pricing needs to be modified by the effects of competition, the presence of any Known Value Items on constant promotion, price lining and what the market will bear.
2. Sales promotions should have clear and, if practicable, measurable objectives.

3. Advertising is not recommended for image building, more for informing customers and potential customers.
4. Public relations, special events and direct mail could all have their place in the promotional portfolio of the smaller retailer.

CHAPTER 8

Purchasing and Inventory Control

Comment has been made throughout the book about how small retailers can develop their 'service' offer to use as a competitive weapon against the multiples. A fundamental element of good service is the ability to provide the goods the customer wants at the time he/she requires them. It is all very well training your staff to be able to describe the features and benefits of your products and recognise buying signals if the goods are not available when the customer makes the decision to buy. Disappointed customers are unlikely to visit your store again. A closely monitored purchasing system is essential to enable a small retailer to meet his customers' needs quickly and accurately.

Whilst retailers Sock Shop and Tie Rack may attribute much of their success to the 'specialist' nature of the products they sell, Kwik Fit the car service company, attribute their phenomenal growth to efficient and effective purchasing and inventory control systems. As mentioned in chapter 1, they began trading in 1971 as a car tyre and accessory shop in Edinburgh, but now have over 350 centres throughout the UK, nearly 100 outlets in France and Holland and are presently planning an international expansion programme for the future. To be able to justify their advertising slogan 'you can't get better than a Kwik Fit fitter' the company have to be certain they carry all the car parts that are required by their customers for all types of motor vehicle. Every Kwik Fit centre is linked electronically to the company's central office which in turn is linked to major suppliers. This way stocks of branded goods are always accessible, and it enables them to offer their widely acclaimed 'While'u'Wait' service.[1]

Although few small retailers can afford the sophisticated computer technology which Kwik Fit have been able to install to control their stock and customer invoicing, the principles behind efficient purchasing systems remain the same and should be applied to any retail operation.

The comments above highlight the importance of purchasing sufficient stock to ensure customers are not lost to the competition because you have run out! Conversely, however, if a small retailer purchases too much stock the business will incur stockholding costs which eat away at the profit figures. Not only could the money tied up in the stock be invested somewhere else and earn a good rate of interest (an opportunity cost), but the stock will require expensive insurance cover and staff to look after it. Money will also be lost through wastage which may occur when the stock does not sell.

Although purchasing decisions are vital to the success of any small retail operation, equally important are the decisions made relating to the storage and control of the stock once on the premises. This chapter will focus on both aspects of the problem.

Purchasing decisions

There are a number of issues a small retailer needs to consider when purchasing goods for the business. *Which* products to buy, the best *place* to buy them from, how *much* to buy and finally how *often* to buy. Each decision needs to be made with the retailer's target market firmly in mind.

Product range decisions: which products to buy

Although this question is normally only discussed in books aimed at small retailers starting up in business, the authors feel the priority placed on product range reviews by large multiples (weekly range review meetings are held in some stores) should be replicated by smaller operators. Range reviews enable retailers to respond more quickly to changes in the market-place. The takeover of Linfoods by Booker Cash and Carry, for example, may have had implications for the product range available to small stores. Unless the retailer is aware of the strengths and weaknesses of their product portfolio he will be unable to decide whether the new ranges are acceptable for his business.

Depth of range

Although ultimately customers dictate what broad range of products or services the small retailer offers, ideas about detailed lines to be included can be generated from a number of sources. A survey of a competitors product range can be useful as a guide, although obviously there is no guarantee that their range will be appropriate for your customers. Even though a competitor may be located only a few streets away, the customer profile may be vastly different. An awareness of the social and demographic characteristics of your trading area is also useful in deciding on the product range.

Because of the costs associated with holding too much stock, a small retailer needs to be careful to avoid carrying too deep a range of products within a line, for example, 10 brands of small canned dog food as was discussed in chapter 6. The retailer in Case Study A made this mistake simply because he wished to make sure none of his customers were disappointed. Although a wide assortment of goods may initially attract customers to the shop, the point is soon reached where the stock becomes jumbled and cluttered and the choice is so bewildering that it no longer becomes an attractive proposition to buy. Figure 8.1 illustrates that there is an optimum assortment of goods where the difference between the costs and the gross profit gives the maximum net profit.

Research into consumer buying behaviour reveals that if the particular variety or product is not available to a customer, the 'need' remains and they are likely to substitute one variety for the other without undue concern. Disappointment arises, however, when the stock is unable to provide any choice within a product range and, even worse, none of the product at all, that is, no dog food at all.

Product profit contribution

Not only should the total range of goods stocked relate to profit calculations, but the smaller retailer must also make an assessment of

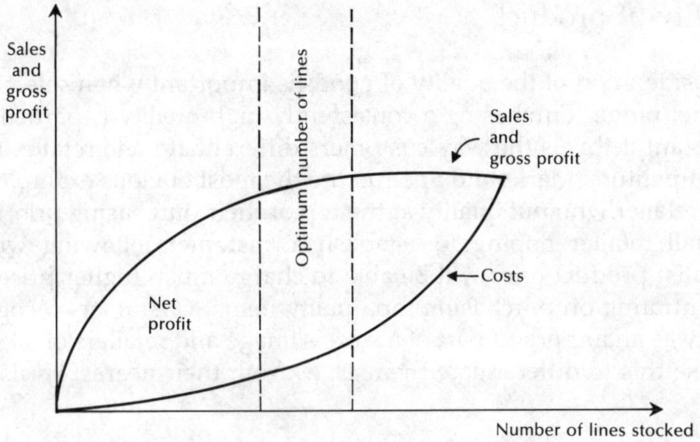

Reproduced with the kind permission of the British Independent Grocers Association

Figure 8.1 Optimum stock assortment

Note: The graph illustrates that, after a certain point, the addition of extra lines to a stock assortment will reduce net profit by increasing costs more than it increases sales and net profit.

the profit contribution each product makes or product category makes. A careful assessment of the profit potential of products will avoid the retailer deciding to delete products from the range based entirely on the frequency of purchase calculation. In Table 8.1 below although the bakery range accounts for only 6.7 per cent of total sales, it makes an above-average contribution to total profit, due to its high margin. Such differences in margin are not uncommon.

Chapter 6 develops this simple idea in more detail in the context of merchandising the range of goods and services on offer.

Table 8.1 Profit contribution of product range

Product	*Turnover per week (£)*	*% of total sales*	*% gross profit*	*£ profit*	*% total profit*
General grocery	5 000	66.6	15	750	49.9
Fruit & veg.	600	8.0	25	150	10.0
Bakery	500	6.7	41	205	13.6
Fresh meat	800	10.7	25	200	13.3
Delicatessen	600	8.0	33	198	13.2
Total	7 500	100.0		1 503	100.0

Quality of product

A consideration of the quality of goods is important when selecting a product range. Purchasing a consistently high quality is particularly important if this is the way customers differentiate one retailer from its competitors. Marks and Spencer are the most obvious example of a large retailer who put quality at the top of their purchasing priorities. A small retailer hoping to establish a customer following with a specialist product offer will be able to charge much higher prices by concentrating on purchasing top quality items. Customers recognise quality as an important part of a store's image and retailers of all sizes can use this to differentiate themselves from their nearest rivals.[2]

The decision on where to purchase

As the multiple operators have demonstrated with the virtual elimination of wholesalers from their distribution network, the ability to offer low prices to customers comes from dealing directly with manufacturers. Transport and storage problems are the major factors preventing smaller operators from reaping these benefits. There are, however, several routes available for small retailers to purchase goods, all of which need to be carefully evaluated and frequently reviewed in the light of the needs of individual businesses.

Cash and Carry operators normally offer small retailers a relatively wide choice of products at wholesale prices in all areas, food, clothing, household goods, and so on. They stock cheaper own-label items as well as the leading brands (own labels include Happy Shopper, Family Choice, and so on). Traditionally no credit facilities were available and retailers were expected to provide their own transport for the goods. Over the past few years, however, competition from other wholesalers appears to have forced many Cash and Carrys to waver their no credit, no delivery policies.

The alternative for grocery bulk purchasing is for a retailer to become affiliated to a *symbol group* trading under a name, for example, Spar. Members pay a service charge in return for certain benefits. These might include advice on store layout and design, advertising, discounts on bulk purchases and negotiated discounts on certain product lines (usually known value items, basic food and household goods) to try to help the smaller operators avoid adverse price comparison against the multiples. Deliveries and credit facilities are available to members. One disadvantage of symbol group membership for the more specialist retailers is that it usually involves making a commitment to purchase certain product lines being promoted within the whole group. In Case Study A for example, the customer profile (foreign and 'yuppie' shoppers) meant that, although the owner could charge premium prices for many product lines, he was under pressure to undercharge simply because the goods were being promoted by the symbol group. The range of products available was also often inappropriate to Mr Bhati's business. There was little demand for the cheaper own-label range of goods, for example, Happy Shopper toilet rolls, but a larger market for specialist products, for example, luxury soft coloured tissues. Cash and Carrys and symbol groups provide an important service for convenience retailers because of the appropriateness of the product range. Symbol groups are also playing a more important role in helping small retailers adopt computerised methods of purchasing and inventory control.

Another alternative for the smaller retailer is to deal *directly with the manufacturer*. Although this may be an expensive method of operating, some retailers have found that a specialist range of a certain product, for example, speciality cheese, can be strategically promoted in store to create customer interest as well as generating an above-average profit contribution. In Case Study A, for example, a daily delivery of croissants from one supplier of continental bread and cakes brought many customers into the store. Once inside they frequently bought more goods.

When trying to evaluate the different methods of processing goods from a financial perspective, small businesses often fail to take into account all the relevant costs. These would include the cost of transport, tax, insurance, petrol etc. as well as the cost of the time spent processing the stock.

How much to purchase

The next question and probably the most important for the small retailer is how much stock to buy over a given period of time. The retailer needs to get the right balance between carrying the financial burden of unsold stock and running out of key lines. One calculation which can be used to restrict the amount of stock taken into a store is based on the idea of Open to Buy (OTB). Open to Buy relates to the amount of new merchandise the retailer can buy in a particular period without exceeding the planned purchases for that period. It represents the difference between what you plan to buy and what is actually bought. The calculations are relatively simple but the information can be very useful in ensuring that regular purchases are not under-ordered. A simple example can be used to illustrate the principle:

A fashion retailer orders long-sleeved blouses Style No. 841 every two weeks. The blouses come directly from A. Bristle & Sons. The manufacturer takes three weeks to deliver the goods. With the exception of seasonal fluctuations, sales of blouses are fairly static, averaging four per week and the retailer sees no reason why this should change in the foreseeable future. Because deliveries are frequently late and there is little storage space at the store the retailer likes to hold two weeks sales in stock.

OTB involves two calculations:

1. Calculate the *maximum inventory*. Add the safety stock (2×4 blouses = 8) to the sales anticipated over the period between orders (2×4 blouses = 8) plus what will be sold in the delivery period (3×4 = 12).
   Maximum inventory = safety stock (8) + order period sales (8) + delivery period sales (12) = 28 blouses. This figure will only form the order size if the present stock level is zero and there are no outstanding orders. If the retailer has some stock or outstanding deliveries these need to be included in the overall calculation of OTB.
2. The final calculation of OTB: maximum inventory – current stock – units on order.
   In this example the retailer had 8 blouses in stock and already had 4 blouses on order. The open to buy figure becomes the order figure OTB = 28 – 8 – 4 = 16 to order.

The major value of this method of inventory control is that it accommodates stock movements, planned stock and periodic reorder points which may not fit in with the sales pattern.

Retailers who closely observe their trading fluctuations can make several adjustments within the formula simply by making additions to the sales and safety figures. The key decisions which operate the system are *estimates of sales* and *safety stock*. Both decisions will alter from one retailer to another depending on the nature of the products and store location.

How often to buy

The frequency of purchase is an important variable a retailer has to consider to achieve the required balance between too much stock and too little. Everything depends upon how quickly a retailer can turn over his stock, that is, his stockturn ratio. The stockturn figure is the ratio expressing the relationship between a retailer's *sales* and the level of average *stock* he has. A number of examples will illustrate the point. The examples are all convenience grocery retailers and therefore their ratios will differ from small businesses handling different product categories (see Table 8.2).

Table 8.2 Stock ratios for three retailers

Retailer (1)	Weekly sales turnover = £ 75 000
	Average stock figure = £300 000
	Number of weeks to turnover stock = 4
Retailer (2)	Weekly sales turnover = £25 000
	Average stock figure = £75 000
	Number of weeks to turnover stock = 3
Retailer (3)	Weekly sales turnover = £ 4 000
	Stockholding = £12 000
	Number of weeks to turnover stock = 3

In Table 8.2 retailers (2) and (3) are controlling their stock more efficiently as the merchandise is being turned over more quickly and money is not held up in dead stock. In stock accounting terms the *stockturn ratio* has a different meaning. Weekly data on stock levels is not usually available and companies are compared on information found in their annual profit and loss accounts and balance sheets. In this case the ratio would read:

$$\frac{\text{Sales for year}}{\text{Average stock figure}} \quad \text{where Average stock figure} =$$

$$\frac{\text{stock at beginning of year} + \text{stock at end}}{2}$$

A simple example £1200/£300 reveals a stockturn of 4. In this example the higher the stockturn ratio the better. Despite the existence of the different calculations, the principle relationship between stock and sales remains the same. As with all ratios the 'stockturn' figure is useful for comparing one business with another provided a consistent method of calculation is used.

The decision about how often to purchase is linked closely to the credit facilities which the small retailer is able to obtain. In Table 8.2, for example, the retailer is able to purchase the majority of his goods on a month's credit with his suppliers. Obviously with his stock turning over in just under four weeks this assures a positive cash flow. As chapter 2 highlights, the small retailer's cash-flow position is an important element in the long-term survival of the business.

The timing and frequency of purchase for many retailers is often influenced by the individual store's trading pattern and staff availability (in theory the two should be organised along the same lines). It is no use arranging to have three fresh-food deliveries to arrive during a peak trading period when there are no staff available to put the merchandise into fridges. Suppliers will understandably place deliveries to larger operators high on their list of priorities, that is, early mornings and early in a week. For this reason small retailers should inform companies well in advance of their delivery requirements and make every effort not to change their pattern very often.

Inventory control

The second half of this chapter will focus on procedures associated with looking after the stock once it has been ordered and received. The key point stressed so far has been that stock in a retailer's store represents money which could be reinvested and earning interest for the retailer elsewhere. Any damage which is done to the merchandise between the time the retailer receives it and when the customer walks out of the store with the goods represents lost profit for the business. Before the advent of computerisation it was certainly easier for a smaller retailer to retain control over the stock at this stage than for a multiple. Whilst the owner/manager would often deal personally with each delivery agent, checking off the merchandise against the delivery notes, querying discrepancies, and so on, larger retailers would have to rely on different employees to book in stock and store it correctly in the warehouse. A large percentage of employee theft in multiples takes place in the vicinity of the 'backdoor'. Although computerised pricing systems have alleviated this problem to some extent, the efficient small retailer can still retain a sole advantage in the area of control. Once again different product categories will require different detailed booking-in systems, but the principles remain the same for all. As common sense implies, the more accurate the checking procedures and the more detailed the documentation, the closer the level of control. Even if the retailer purchases all the goods from a Cash and Carry and collects it himself, a booking-in system is still required to ensure that everything paid for comes out of the premises.

FIFO and LIFO

Once inside the store a number of stock control principles can be applied. First, FIFO and LIFO (first in and first out and last in and first out). FIFO means that the retailer sells stock in date order of purchase. Almost every grocery product, for example, whether long or short life now bears some indication on the product packaging about the length of time it can safely be kept by the retailer before being consumed. This may take the form of either a sell-by date or, in the case of canned products, a production date. The small retailer needs to pay particular attention to these dates for two reasons. First, because it is a criminal offence punishable by a fine or imprisonment to sell substandard merchandise of any description (Food Act 1984; Consumer Safety Amendment Act 1986). Undercover Trading Standards and Environmental Health officials make frequent checks on small retail outlets and accept no excuses for badly-rotated stock. Secondly, because of the damage that can be done to the retailer's reputation with customers.

The trend towards healthy eating and the existence of a more educated and discerning customer has meant that customers take a much closer interest within stores in the nature of the products they are purchasing. Although price is important to some customers, quality has become a far more influential element in the purchase decision. This idea is confirmed by a recent survey of retail customers designed to test their awareness of price differentials between stores and branded products. 10 000 interviews were carried out with customers before they entered supermarkets. Forty per cent of interviewees were unable to give estimates of the prices they would be charged for the goods and 20 per cent thought prices would be higher than they actually were. The report makes a note of the fact that products were chosen for quality rather than price.[3] Customers in today's retail environment are prepared to spend a little longer in store examining sell-by-dates and reading nutritional information and no longer can small retailers be comforted by the idea that customers chose the first goods that come to hand.

Small clothing retailers also need to appy the FIFO principle in stock control if they are to keep apace with seasonal variations in demand. The tightening up of Consumer Protection Legislation in Britain (given impetus by the involvement of the European Commission) has led to much stricter regulations governing 'sale' items and special offers in stores. Although traditionally a method of attracting customers into a store, many small retailers use sales as an excuse for badly-organised inventory control systems.

LIFO is the alternative system to FIFO and means last in first out. Fresh stock is sold before old stock of the same line.

Stock record cards

One of the major objectives of inventory control systems are to give the retailer an accurate assessment of fast- and slow-moving items within the store. As has already been pointed out, the initial overview of sales needs to be accompanied by an analysis of the profit contribution each product makes. In reality, however, many small retailers do not appear to have adequate documentation to give a detailed sales breakdown of products, let alone carry out a contribution analysis. The author's view is that the situation in Case Study A is typical rather than atypical of many small-scale operators. The manager/owner is likely to have quite detailed knowledge of fast and slow sellers and average sales per week of key lines, but stored in one person's memory rather than documented, and obtained from 'gut' feel and experience of working in the store rather than calculation. The situation can be compared to that in Case Study B where a good deal of product data was gathered.

Accurate sales information is fundamental for the smaller retailer before any of the principles of store layout, stocking, pricing, and so on, outlined in the book can be applied. Once again computerised stock control packages which break down sales data from the tills and link it to reordering systems are widely available for the smaller retailer and will be discussed in more depth in chapter 10. However small retailers who claim they do not have the money to invest in such systems should still be operating some form of manual check operation which will yield much of the sales data required. The basic principles remain the same.

A stock record card can form a part of a manual check system. The card is simply a record of stock and sales information and ideally should be held for each product line (or category). The manual system obviously involves labour to fill in the card on a regular basis, but because it is a very simple device all employees can be trained on how to fill one in. In Figure 8.2 below the product stock level is counted every week. Obviously if this is too time consuming the retailer can complete the card every two weeks, every month or even every six weeks, but the more frequently the information is recorded the greater the level of control. Cards can be stored in index files if computer support is not available. The precise amount of information contained on each card can be left to the discretion of individual retailers and Figure 8.2 just gives one type of example for a line of children's trousers.

PRODUCT DESCRIPTION : TROUSERS LS24											
DATE	OPENING STOCK			ON ORDER	DELIVERIES	DATE	CLOSING STOCK			SALES
	SR	SF	Total		Received		SR	SF	Total	
12.9.88	12	12	24	20	12 SD	15.9	14	10	24	12
19.9.88	14	10	24	10	10	22.9	10	9	19	15
26.9.88	10	9	19	20	15 SD	28.9	10	7	17	17
3.10.88	10	7	17	26	26	6.10	15	12	27	16

SR = Stock Room SF = Sales Floor SD = Short Delivery

Figure 8.2 A stock record card

The 'on order' column can be included with information transferred from advice notes. Staff can then refer to the cards to inform customers whether products are likely to be received in the near future. Other information which could be included is historic sales data, that is, the sales record of the particular line over the same period last year. This can prove to be particularly useful when a small retailer is planning order quantities for seasonal increases like Christmas. The information also tells you how reliable your present delivery system is. A regular check on short and over deliveries gives the small retailer bargaining power when negotiating new orders with suppliers.

It should be stressed that all the above data would ideally be stored on a computer database. Although few independents claim to have the financial resources available in 1988 to purchase the necessary hardware and software, the situation in ten years time will be very different. Small retailers may be forced to change their methods of control over the business and adapt the major ideas currently being developed by the multiples.

Stocktaking

The ideal time for implementing a stock control system based on stock record cards would perhaps be directly after the business's stocktake. The stocktake involves the retailer making a full count of all products within the store. It usually takes place once or twice a year and consists of a calculation of the value of all stock at a certain period in time at the cost price. Accurate period-end stock counting is essential to verify the annual profit calculation for the business. The normal method of stocktaking in a small retail outlet would be to first record the selling price and the number of goods at that price in stock. The selling price would then be marked down to cost (the markdown often being the retailer's average gross profit margin less some margin for unknown loss, that is, shrinkage). Stocktaking is a time-consuming exercise for all retailers because of the wide variety of merchandise to be taken into account. The key to success lies in careful preparation. Stocktaking sheets should be drawn up and all goods made easy to count and clearly marked with their selling price. VAT can then be deducted from the gross value to give the total net value of the stock. Obviously it follows that if the retailer has been operating an efficient stock counting system on a regular basis, the six-monthly or annual check will cause no difficulties. The annual stocktake is a more formal appraisal of stock than the count of items needed to maintain a stock record card. The value of stock must be known for the annual accounts.

Negotiating with suppliers

The final area which needs more mention under a chapter entitled Purchasing and Inventory Control is the importance to the smaller retailer of developing good negotiating skills. Making sure that you have not overpurchased in total volume is one matter, but making sure that you are buying at the keenest possible price is another. Obviously the amount of leeway you have in price negotiations will depend upon who you are dealing with and the order quantity involved. A smaller specialist manufacturer may have the flexibility to give various discounts to retailers, but if the product range occupies a good position in a niche market he may have no incentive to do so. Although by obtaining a good cost price a smaller retailer can logically offer attractive retail prices to customers, the key themes running throughout the book has been that small operators should not over emphasise competing on price. The same idea applies when negotiating deals with suppliers. The smaller retailer should concentrate on the other elements in the 'deal', for example, product quality. Small suppliers have to take back legally substandard goods, but to avoid unnecessary disputes a retailer might consider building in his own quality standard definitions into the contract. Similarly, negotiating help with promotion and display on a long-term basis can prove more valuable to a strategically positioned business than a few extra pence off the average cost price. This would undoubtedly be a more sensible approach for the retailer in Case Study A. While his customers would not be put off if he charged more for a wide range of products in the store, he needs help to implement stock control systems and plans for merchandise layout. Both could be obtained from negotiations with suppliers.

A successful negotiation in psychological terms occurs when both parties feel that they have something valuable from the discussion – a win-win situation. Heated arguments do nothing to develop long-term relationships which can hold the key to success for a small retailer. An atmosphere of trust and loyalty needs to be built up so that the retailer can be sure the supplier will be sympathetic to his problems and not stop supplying goods at the first mention of a better price somewhere else.

Finally, even though a retail business may be small compared to the multiple operators, the independent should always try to approach the person actually responsible for making a decision within the supplier's organisation. There is always a tendency for smaller negotiations to be handled by agents who rarely have the authority to take any real decisions. A retailer may find he has wasted a great deal of valuable time speaking to the wrong person.

This chapter has concentrated on two areas – *purchasing* (range selection, quality and timing) and *manual inventory control* (looking at stock record cards and stocktaking procedures). Although mention has been made of the growing importance of computerisation in this area, the authors have chosen to focus on this in a little more detail in chapter 10. The justification for this in a book on small retailers lies in the dichotomy between what stock control systems owner/managers *could* and *ought* to have in their small business and what they *do* have in reality.

Keypoint summary

1. Purchasing and inventory control is important to the smaller retailer for two reasons:
   - to be able to provide an efficient service;
   - to avoid unnecessary stockholding costs.
2. Purchasing decisions involve:
   - deciding on a range of products which optimises net profit whilst giving quality and variety to the customer;
   - choosing the best source of supply;
   - deciding on the volume of product to be purchased (by applying the OTB principle);
   - deciding on the frequency of purchase (using a stockturn ratio).
3. Procedures for the storage and handling of stock involve the application of some or all of the following ideas: stock rotation (FIFO), records of stock, sales and order data and stocktaking.
4. An awareness of negotiating skills can help the smaller retailer

obtain help from suppliers unrelated to price, for example, promotion and merchandising assistance.

5. The application of computer inventory control systems is crucial to the long-term success of the smaller retailer but presently few appear to have the financial resources to implement them.

CHAPTER 9

The People Dimension

'People and personal relations are the key to success in running the small enterprise'[1]

How true this is for the small retail business today. This chapter will look at the nature of relationships within small retail operations with the aim of showing the reader how the 'people' in the organisation, if handled correctly, can be used as an effective weapon in the independent's battle against the multiples. The comments will be divided into two. First, a discussion of the *employees* within the business, and secondly, what could be referred to as the *'Entrepreneurs' or owner managers'*. Although retail owners frequently take a very active role in the day-to-day operation of the business, if they are sole traders or partnerships they are clearly differentiated from their employees and display marked differences in terms of job motivation.

Before undertaking any detailed analysis of the small retailer's position, an overview of the trends and issues in retail employment generally will help to place later comments in context.

The background: employment in retailing

According to various government sources of data, over 2 million people in Britain are employed in retailing today. Although there appears to be uncertainty about the overall contribution that retailing makes to job creation, the fact that retailers employ such a substantial number of workers means that they can have an enormous social impact through their employment policies.[2]

The major developments regarding the composition of the retail labour force can be easily observed in the market-place and apply to both small and large retail sectors:

1. The increase in the number of *part-time* employees as a percentage of the total retail labour force (46 per cent in 1976 to 54 per cent in 1986).
2. The increase in the number of *female* employees in the industry, 66 per cent of the total labour force now being women. As Spark's[3] research illustrates, the feminisation of the retail work-force, (increasing since the early 1960s) has been most evident in the part-time sector.

The attraction of part-time workers for retail employers relates largely to the increased flexibility it gives them in coping with fluctuating staffing requirements. The problem is greater in retailing due to the rapidly increasing length of the trading week and the pattern of customer flow, heavily peaked in terms of days. An additional incentive for the cost-conscious small retailer to employ part-timers is the avoidance of certain legal obligations and restrictions, for example, part-time staff working less than a 16-hour week do not have to be given a contract of employment unless they have been employed continuously for 8 or more hours a week for at least 5 years.

Female part-time workers find this form of work more suitable as it allows them to combine family responsibilities with paid employment. Sparks links the increase in the number of females in the retail labour force with the move to 'out-of-town' retailing of the large multiples. Retailers, he feels, have been able to tap into the suburban female labour force conveniently located within the catchment area of the superstores.[4]

Composition of the labour force

Another change of particular relevance to the composition of the labour force in the smaller retail sector is the increasing participation of *ethnic minorities*, more specifically 'Asians', in retail operations. About 60 per cent of Asian firms in Britain are in retail distribution. Ward estimated that in 1985 12 per cent of all independent retail outlets in Britain were Asian owned.[5] Although more recent statistics have not been collated, the authors estimate the figure to be nearer 20 per cent in 1988.

The composition of the labour force in small retail outlets is also characterised by a large percentage of *family employees*. An unpublished survey of 15 successful independent retail grocery outlets revealed that, including husband and wife teams, as much as 46 per cent of the labour force were related in some form or another. One of the owners in the survey commented that he felt strong family involvement was essential to ensure success. This form of labour has very obvious advantages to the retailer as is evident from Case Study A. A major constraint on business growth was the lack of potential employees he felt he could trust. Trust within a family is something which is taken for granted and relieves any anxieties about staff theft and absenteeism. Large retailers like Marks and Spencer also recognise the qualities of employees who are related to each other and place the issue high on the list of priorities in their selection procedure. A question on an application form is aimed specifically at finding out if candidates are related to anyone currently employed in the organisation. A positive response, in the authors' opinion, undoubtedly increases the candidate's chance of success.

Other writers have commented on the existence of a high proportion of younger, less-well-qualified, less stable employees in a small business versus older, well qualified and experienced workers with a stable work history in larger outlets.[6] Although problems in defining small retailers outlined in chapter 1 makes it difficult to collect detailed evidence of this in retailing outlets, the survey of 15 independents mentioned earlier revealed a high percentage of employees under 20 years old. Because small retailers cannot usually match the reward packages offered by the multiples in terms of wages, fringe benefits or opportunities for career mobility, it would seem logical that they would attract younger, less-well-qualified employees. The problem for the small retailer of being able to afford to offer competitive salaries to shopworkers is one of the reasons for interest in providing 2-year work placements for YTS trainees, where the Training Commission subsidise the retailer for the wages paid to the employee in return for a formal commitment to continued employee training. A good employer should provide continued training for *all* employees, irrespective of age or qualifications. Consequently, the YTS scheme can be used as an excellent recruitment ground for the small retailer.

Employees as a competitive weapon against the multiples

Employees form a critical part of the 'service offer' which the small retailer can develop to generate a competitive advantage over the large multiples. Despite heavy investment by the multiple retailers in 'customer care' programmes, evidence suggests that customers still remain dissatisfied with the standard of personal attention they receive in stores, unless multiples can invest heavily in training. In 1988 Gateway attempted to improve the situation with their 'people first' scheme designed to bring all the company's 66 800 employees up to one set standard of service. This scheme involved 90 days of instruction for *all* store staff and managers and consequently proved to be a very costly operation.

A common excuse which comes back from retailers to explain their poor service standards usually focuses on the lack of finance available to pay for sufficient staff to provide personal service for each individual customer.

The argument can be counteracted in two ways:

First, as there appears to be sufficient funds available to invest in *store* refurbishment (an *Economist* survey of September 1986 found that of 54 of the UKs largest retailers, three-quarters had begun modernising their stores in the previous two years, and half of the remainder intended to do so).[7] The issue appears to be one of priorities. What do large retailers view as more important investment in buildings/structures or investment in people?

Secondly, the standard of service is determined more by the *quality of training* given to employees rather than the quantity, that is, the number of staff available. The solution in many cases is not to try to take on more employees but to improve the frequency and standard of service training.

Service as a competitive advantage

The authors' view is that the small retail business is in a far better position to be able to provide the high standard of service increasingly demanded by customers.

Although physical working conditions in the small firm may be inferior, communication channels are often more open and employees can see the relation between what they are doing and the objectives and performance of the firm as a whole more easily. From the authors' own experience, retail employees in small outlets certainly appear to be more interested in providing quality service for customers.

A questionnaire filled in by 200 retail YTS trainees receiving their 'off-the-job' training at Bilston Community College of Further Education revealed some very obvious information to back up this idea. Trainees attended the college one day each week to receive the 'theoretical' input on retailing to complement the training received at their work placements on the other days. The majority of these placements were in small retail outlets, for example, florists, greengrocers, shoe shops and insurance agencies. When asked the simple question 'which aspect of your work placement did you enjoy most?', 90 per cent expressed the same idea in one form or another – the time spent talking to customers and helping them to find the right product. Their worst experiences ranged from cleaning the floor to sexual harassment at the workplace, but the point comes across quite clearly. They demonstrated a desire to communicate with customers and help them to satisfy their needs in a retail context, a desire which small retailers can quickly capitalise on.

When training employees the emphasis should be on *quality* inputs. A simple course on sales training is essential to enable employees to recognise buying signals being transmitted by customers and convert them into profitable sales and happy customers.

Feedback and encouragement are also vital to success, and the owner/manager is well placed to monitor the progress of employees.

Incentive schemes relating to customer service activities are particularly effective in a retailing environment. One small hairdressing outlet had a staffing structure based on the concept of juniors/stylists and directors. Progression to director was made purely on the basis of the number of customers who asked for their hair to be cut by the named individual over a specified period of time. An employee's 'success' depended on the relative number of satisfied customers gained.

There is evidence to indicate that many small retailers are already exploiting the 'service' advantage. A recent television documentary profiling customer shopping habits highlighted the ability of the staff of a small retailer to create a more 'satisfied' customer simply by talking carefully to them and matching their needs closely to the products available.

Five 'shoppers' were asked on the programme where they went for the majority of their food shopping. The interviewees were female, and were drawn from a broad cross-section of society. The women inevitably identified different multiples for their 'bulk' purchases, but all five stated that they still purchased meat from their local, small butcher. The women were unanimous in their justification 'because he knows exactly what my family likes, lean or cheaper cuts and will only give me the amount I ask for'. Other comments indicated that the butcher knew a great deal about the women's families and likes/dislikes which did not relate specifically to the product being sold. Although it could be argued that the butcher has more immediate control over product modification than some small outlets, he/she still demonstrated the same qualities – the ability to establish customer needs closely and tailor them to the product available.

The small retailer has a greater opportunity through training to develop this skill in *all* employees than a highly bureaucratic and automated multiple retailer. Satisfied customers lead to repeat purchases so critical to the survival of the small retailer.

The importance of staff training is emphasised by John Gallanders the owner of a Spar grocer outlet near Wrexham. Much of the success of the £9000 per week store he attributed to employee loyalty and service. Staff training received a high priority. 'Being small does not mean we should neglect the development of our people' he commented. Using Spar training cassettes, John held training sessions three mornings per week for his staff, the main emphasis being on developing good customer relations.[8]

Staff as a business cost

Common sense indicates that employing people can, if handled badly, cost the employer time, money or lost profitability. As has already been noted for the majority of small retail businesses, wage costs can represent anything up to one-third of total costs and are therefore an important element in the retail cost-control system. Although a contented, motivated work-force is the ideal, a small retailer cannot afford to lose control of the financial aspects of employment. Newby comments on the dilemma faced by the smaller business with the financial issue, and that people have to get along with each other. Indeed, the moral involvement of those involved is an important internal resource of the enterprise. But, on the other hand, external market influences on the enterprise dictate that profit and loss considerations must take first place over any personal and social relations.[9]

Staffing requirements need to be closely monitored and costed. Inadequate staff cover not only leads to poor customer service, with no one on the tills, half-empty shelves, and harassed unfriendly staff, but employees under pressure also tend to make more errors whether operating the till or pricing stock. These factors and a stressful atmosphere result in lost custom and profit. Overstaffing can also cause problems, however. Work tends to expand to fill the time available, staff soon become bored and lose interest in their work. To ensure that staffing requirements are controlled 'Purchase in, Talking shop' recommends that the trader should draw up a 'Trading Plan'. The Plan consists of details of delivery times and peak trading periods to try to ensure these coincide with staff availability.

The question of motivation

This chapter so far has highlighted two major points relating to employees in a small retail business: first, the importance of training staff in customer-selling techniques to enable the business to exploit the 'service offer' in the face of multiple competition; secondly, the need to recognise employees as a business cost, necessitating close and constant monitoring and control. A small retailer who focuses on these two areas will go a long way to achieving the ideal of a motivated work-force. Employees will feel valued by the emphasis on training and feedback and will receive wages commensurate with their performance.

Another major motivating factor for employees relates to the concept of 'fair' treatment in the workplace. The lack of union activity characteristic of small retail businesses makes it very important for employees to feel that the employer is abiding by the *legal* regulations which protect their position within the organisation. Two studies by the Policy Studies Institute in 1978 and the Department of Employment in 1979 reported that in the 301 small firms they had studied, the owner/manager's knowledge of employment legislation was often far from complete.

Excellent coverage of all employment legislation relevant to the small retail business is outlined in the *1988/1989 British Independent Grocers' Association Yearbook*.[11] The 33 pages devoted to the subject are divided into the following areas: Recruitment, the period of employment, termination of the period of employment or dismissal, redundancy and safety. Although the legal section is particularly comprehensive, the association also provides discounts for small retailers on insurance matters, a debt collection service and advice on business operation problems, as well as current information relating to nationally-negotiated minimum wage rates. For a small fee the association will also send retailers standard legal documents relating to employment issues to ease the burden of administration for the small retailer, for example, a contract of employment.

Another good source of information is the Advisory, Conciliation and Arbitration Service *ACAS Handbook for Small Firms* entitled 'Employing People' which is available free from any ACAS Regional Office.[12] Both these documents provide the information a small retailer needs to keep his employment policies on the right side of the law. For this reason these pieces of legislation will not receive attention specifically in this book.

There is one area, however, of a more contentious nature which affects small retailers when employing and dismissing staff which is often neglected in the literature. The issue of discrimination. Over the past 20 years public awareness of, and interest in, the area of discrimination has increased to such an extent that no employer, large or small, can dismiss it as irrelevant to their business. Put simply, it relates to the situation where an employer or prospective employer treats one person less favourably than another because of that person's sex, race, colour, ethnic, national origin or marital status. In legal terms discrimination can take on one of four forms:

1. *Direct discrimination*, for example, in an advertisement such as: WAREHOUSE STAFF REQUIRED, ASIANS NEED NOT APPLY (that is, directly excluding one group).
2. *Indirect discrimination*, for example, ALL APPLICANTS MUST BE 65 AND HAVE A BEARD (implying that unless women suddenly grow beards they will not be eligible).
3. *Victimisation*, for example, taking disciplinary action against an employee because he/she has a case against you being heard by an Industrial Tribunal.
4. *Segregation*, for example, staff room 'A' to be used by European staff, staff room 'B' by Asian staff.

Discrimination is unlawful in *any* of these areas of employment – recruitment, the period of employment or when a person is dismissed. The pieces of legislation being contravened are the *Sex Discrimination Act 1975* and the *Race Relations Act 1976* and the laws are monitored by the Equal Opportunities Commission and the Race Relations Board. The outcome of an investigation by either body on a retailer could be a fine of up to £2000 if found guilty, or compensation for an employee of up to a maximum of £8500 if taken before an Industrial Tribunal.

Discrimination and the 'small' retailer

Although the amount of money a small retailer could lose is significant, more damage could be done to the smaller business's 'image'

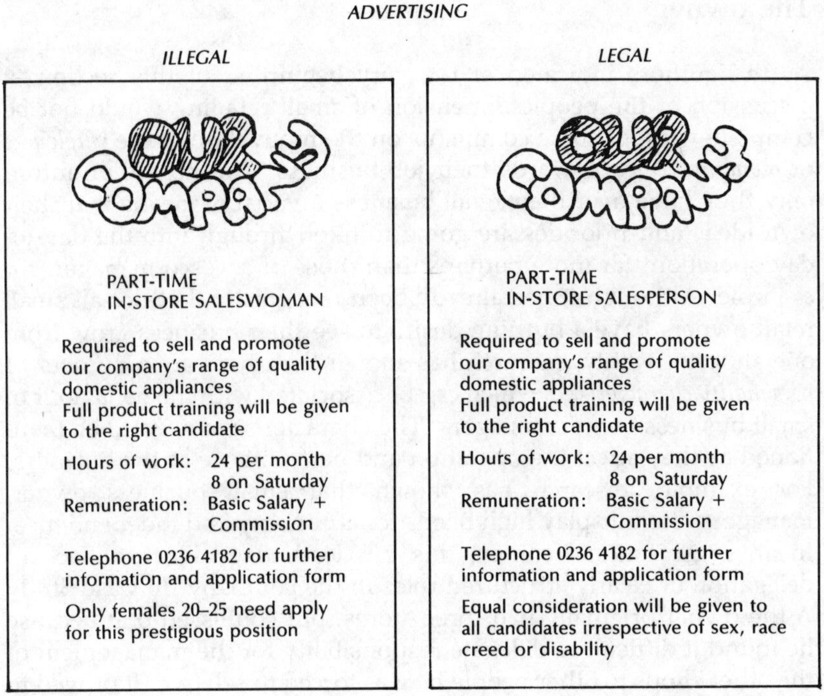

Figure 9.1 Examples of illegal and legal advertisement

from adverse publicity. Newspapers are always ready to publicise cases of employment discrimination, and for a smaller retailer whose reputation in the community is often one of the key ingredients to his success, adverse coverage could prove to be particularly damaging.

Two of the most obvious ways a small retailer may be caught out are when *advertising* for (see Figure 9.1), and *interviewing*, new employees.

As can be seen from Figure 9.1, any advertisement will fall foul of the law if it contains words with a sexual connotation which would be taken as an indication to discriminate. The inclusion of the phrase *an equal opportunity employer* makes doubly sure the law has not been contravened.

Interviewing

If a woman or coloured person, for example, can establish that they were not given a job at the interview stage because of the manner in which the interview was conducted or the type of questions asked, then they may well have a case to take to an industrial tribunal.

The owner

As the authors indicated at the very beginning of this section, a discussion of the people dimension of small retailing would not be complete without some comments on the motivation of the *employers* or *owner/managers* towards their job business. The degree of autonomy they have over their retail business invariably means that their own ideas and priorities are going to filter through into the day-to-day operation, far more perhaps than those of a Tesco manager, for example. Although it has already been recognised that not all small retail owners have a burning desire to see their business grow from one shop to twenty, research has shown that there are a number of *personality characteristics* which can be associated with the behaviour of small business owner/managers. The characteristics need to be mentioned as they affect the operation and performance of the business. For example, research has shown that small business owner/managers often display high needs for autonomy and independence. In an organisational context this can lead to evidence of lack of delegation or clearly-structured roles in the company. In Case Study A the owner originally had three stores, but confessed that because he found it difficult to delegate responsibility for the management of the other shops to other people he was forced to sell two. It proved to be a physical impossibility to run all three himself.

Conversation with small retail owners in many areas soon reinforces the idea that 'active participation' in the daily operation of the business is what provides them with job (and life) satisfaction.

Situational factors are also important determinants of employer motivation in small retail operations. The pressure to maintain standards of family life is undoubtedly the major driving force behind the owner in Case Study A. Others which spring to mind include a desire or pressure to combine a family tradition of retail business. There are also owners who have found themselves with a redundancy payment and few job specific skills, and have decided to embark upon a career in retailing.

Although more could be said about 'employer' motivation in small-scale retailing, there is always a danger of over-generalising about patterns of behaviour. The important point to note is that the small retailer's motivation towards his business is *more likely to have a direct daily impact on the running of the operation* than is the case with a large retailer owner. Although the personality of Terence Conran in control of the Storehouse Group may have had a visible impact on the operation of BHS, the size and diversity of the organisation he controls makes it very difficult to have a similar influence on other parts of the group, particularly in the short term.

Keypoint summary

1. Changes in retail employment include an increase in part-time women employees.
2. Employment in small-scale retailing is characterised by family employees, ethnic minorities (Asians) and younger employees.
3. Employees are more important to small retailers as a strategic weapon against multiples and as a major cost to the business.
4. An understanding of the legal constraints and issues surrounding retail employment are important for three reasons: (1) to avoid unnecessary legal costs, (2) to let employees believe they are being treated fairly, (3) to avoid adverse publicity.
5. The motivation of the small retail employer is important as it affects daily business operation directly.

CHAPTER 10

Methods of Control

The main controls in retailing are common to all types and size of retailer. Every retailer looks to make a trading profit. That profit will need to be large enough to satisfy the owners, be they shareholders or a husband and wife. A satisfactory profit is normally one that provides an income from the investment by the owners that compares well enough with an income by placing the investment elsewhere.

Both types of owner will assess income from profit and growth in the value of the business when judging how well the business is doing. Both will be concerned that the future financial needs of the business are included in their assessment, for example, that the profit is large enough to cover future refurbishment costs.

The main concepts in financial management are covered in chapter 11. This chapter aims to discuss a number of secondary control criteria that can be used to assess a retail business, so-called performance criteria.

Sales performance criteria

In the chapters on merchandising and store design, the idea of assessing the contributing parts of the store to the business as a whole by making each product pay a rental charge was introduced. Sales per

Table 10.1 Reasons behind inadequate criteria

Criterion	*Potential reason for poor performance*
Sales per square foot	Lack of stock Poor location Lack of advertising Strong competition Fundamental problem with retail offer Poor/disorganised layout
Sales per employee	Most of the above reasons Poor staff training Poor staff control Too many staff Staff available at the wrong time (poor staff planning)
Sales per customer	Poor merchandise mix Too small a product range Inadequate selling by staff Illogical layout of shop Not enough specialisation/authority in product offer Too crowded a shop Price competition on major lines

square foot is one of the major performance criteria used in retailing. The performance of individual products or parts of the store can be compared to identify poor performers and emphasise lines with greater potential. The sales per square foot measure achieved by other retailers in the same line of business could serve as a useful comparison if such data were available. Larger retailers publish such data in their annual reports, smaller retailers might be willing to discuss such figures privately.

Coupled with sales per square foot are sales per employee and sales per customer. A poor performance against any of these figures might just imply a poor overall performance because the shop is just not attractive enough. However, identifying a poor performance in just one of these may lead to a weakness being uncovered that can be rectified. Table 10.1 lists some of the factors that may be causing a problem in any one area.

A comparison with another retailer is always useful, but so is an attempt to improve one or more of each sales performance figures. There is no harm in letting staff know what is being aimed for. Retail employees frequently complain about a lack of clear guidance from management. Encouraging employee participation in attaining improvements in key performance criteria could be advisable.

Customer flow and walkout

The number of customers entering a shop indicates how good the retailer's image is in the market-place. A low or declining flow implies the retailer either lacks differentiation from any local competition, or the retail offer is not attractive enough to a large enough group of customers if there is no competition.

Advertising is one answer to the second issue and a radical re-thinking of the business the only answer to the first. A retailer with a poor location may also suffer from poor customer flow, but promotion should be capable of countering some disadvantages here. Too poor a location and the necessary promotional budget will be too high to achieve profitability.

A good external image but a poor delivery of that image in store causes a high walkout rate. Someone has been attracted to the store but leaves without purchasing. Walkout rates vary by type of business. High fashion shops may have a 50 or 70 per cent walkout, while a food retailer might see as little as 5 per cent.

A larger shop can analyse its walkout rate by department. A department with a high share of walkouts compared to its share of turnover can have a merchandise problem. Quite probably the departmental buyer has bought with a different view of the shop's external image from that of other buyers and certainly of customers. Customers may well assess a department store on the basis of its fashion offer and, based on this, form an opinion of what the China-wear offer would be, only to discover their mistake and leave disappointed. Other customers, with the same expectation of the Chinawear offer might never visit.

Coherence in a multiproduct store's image is important unless each department can establish its own identity to customers.

The walkout rate of a shop or of individual departments can be measured by means of a survey. Customers leaving the store are asked whether they made a purchase. Those who did not are asked which departments they visited and why. A high percentage of people leaving, having planned to buy rather than browse, could be a sign of problems that need rapid attention.

EFTPOS

Electronic Funds Transfer at Point Of Sale (EFTPOS) looked as if it would never be a practical reality because of disputes between retailers and bankers as to who should pay for the service. It was generally recognised that customers would be unlikely to accept a charge for the priviledge of having their money taken from their accounts faster than by cheque, or a credit or charge card that allowed a period of free credit.

At the time of writing the problem seemed to have been resolved, and pilot studies with systems such as Midland Banks Midnight Express with retailers of all sizes appear encouraging, offering better control over cash for the retailer.[1]

Margin control

Some retailers plan and control on the basis of gross profit, the difference between buying and selling prices, some on net profit, including a fair allocation for variable and fixed costs. The latter is more precise in theory but more complex and difficult to make accurate as assumptions have to be made about cost allocations.

Shrinkage levels

Shrinkage is the difference between the revenue that *should* have been received and what was *actually* received. Some stock is not converted to its expected revenue because:

1. It was not actually delivered.
2. It was broken or spoiled.
3. It was stolen.
4. It was marked down.

In addition, shrinkage can occur by direct theft of cash or fraud by customers in submitting bad cheques or stolen cheques.

It is claimed that two-thirds of shrinkage is due to staff theft and a quarter to shoplifting. Sometimes apparent shrinkage is due to error, goods that were apparently delivered being left on vans or mistakes in stock counts, but more often the problem is a real one. Some stores suffer losses of around 5 per cent of turnover, most retailers budget for substantial sums that are never accounted for.

Laying down clear procedures in the receiving of goods; making sure employees are aware of the consequences of any personal misdemeanour; seeking the advice of the local crime prevention officer on security matters – are all important for any retailer, especially the shopowner who is new to retailing and possibly naïve about the potential damage that can be caused by shrinkage.

Capturing data

The evidence suggests that few entrepreneurs are very analytical about their businesses. This chapter has been largely about using data to analyse a business. Most of the data can be captured for analysis using the two devices of a till receipt and a stock card. Together they provide all the sales and stock data that a retailer needs to control the business.

Some retail businesses fail because they do not use data well enough, some do not even gather the basic data. They rely upon a gut feel on how the business is going. Often it is only the intervention of the VAT inspector or the company's accountant that produces any reliable accounting system.

Kimball tags have been mentioned earlier when discussing ticketing. Their main value to the retailer is as a method of capturing information on what has been sold. The system has its drawbacks, the cost of the tags, the possibility of loss, the cost of ticketing. Bar codes, pre-printed onto product packaging, offer a simpler alternative that is more useful on packaged goods.

By 1987, 70 per cent by volume of turnover of packaged groceries were bar coded. Each item has a unique number conforming to the European Article Number system. The number is represented by a series of marks and spaces offering millions of permutations.

Each bar code can be read automatically by a laser scanner, even if the bar code is not perfectly flat or well positioned as it passes through the reader.

Electronic Point of Sale (EPOS) is still relatively new. Less than 10 stores had EPOS equipment in 1982. By 1986 the idea was beginning to take off and over 400 stores had EPOS equipment. But compared to the 36 000 food stores in Britain, EPOS had a long way to go before it became standard equipment. Nevertheless, by 1995 it is estimated by one source that 80 per cent of packaged goods will be sold through an EPOS system.[2] Another source estimates nearly 40 per cent of all stores by 1995.[3]

Retailers carrying EPOS will tend initially to be the larger stores of the larger chains, but smaller units such as those under the Victor Value, Shopper's Paradise and Bejam names have been to the fore in adopting scanning.

The benefits of EPOS

A survey for ICL in 1986 identified stock control as the third most important benefit from EPOS after better information and better control. Some reduction in shrinkage was also implied. Studies of cost-benefit analyses are hard to come by. One report from McKinsey put benefits at 0.27 per cent of sales from a medium-sized supermarket. NCR estimated that a supermarket in the USA with a turnover of $150 000 a week could save $50 000 a year from the elimination of checkout errors alone, some 0.5 per cent of sales.[4]

Larger retailers tend to emphasise the information benefits of EPOS in controlling their businesses. Certainly the larger the retail company becomes, the more important it is to have good data and to get it quickly. But what of the smaller retailer? Will the electronic revolution reach the independent sector? One independent with two grocery stores had identified a simpler system than that used in most multiple stores, selling at £8050, for two tills, two hand scanners, a computer, printer and software.[5] Other systems were on offer at between £6000 and £15 000. The retailer gave the advantages of EPOS as 'faster throughput at the checkouts, greater accuracy and vastly improved data'. The improvement in data was expected to lead to 'better stock selection, space allocation and ordering'.

The better data that can be expected includes:

Sales by individual product line item
Sales by customer
Sales by time period
Sales by payment type
Sales per checkout

If delivery data and stock data can be fed into the computer, reorder quantities can be calculated automatically. Some larger chains are already experimenting with using this data for automatic reordering of stock from manufacturers. The savings from lower stock levels and fewer stockouts must be more valuable than those reported earlier from better shrinkage and error control.

The largest financial benefit to a retailer is potentially the cost of price-marking goods. Most EPOS systems print out an itemised receipt for the customer with the prices accessed from the linked computer system. As the scanner rarely makes errors in reading the unique bar code for each product, checkout bills tend to be more accurate. Some shoppers are suspicious of the absence of price marked products to check against the till receipt but consumer resistance here seems to be slight.

With an EPOS system the technology exists to make the price displays on the shelves electronic and matched to the price file in the store computer. Prices can be changed instantaneously, possibly even during the day and back again the following day, with prices rising in the late evening to reflect the extra costs of late opening.

Should the smaller retailer adopt EPOS?

The answer to the question is, in most instances, not yet, but sooner or later, yes, in one form or another. The retailer with a large number of stock items, such as a grocery, DIY shop and a chemist, should consider the type of system currently being installed in supermarkets. These will fall in price and increase in sophistication quite rapidly.

Retailers with a moderate number of stock items, but a lower rate of unit sale such as fashion shops, shoe shops, pet shops, china shops (but probably not fresh foods such as greengrocers, florists, butchers, bakers and fishmongers) should consider hand-held Portable Data Captive Units (PDCU) of the kind marketed by MSI or Telxon. With these a product code is typed into a portable keyboard each time a sale is made. This captures the sales data for later input into the computer.

Some retailers do not need to consider EPOS but should not ignore the other benefits of electronics and computerisation in other parts of their business – the travel agent for access to information systems and the Interflora shop for messages are as just two examples of what is already in use.

Keypoint summary

1. Various commercial controls can be applied in retailing from financial ones such as sales per square foot to marketing ones such as customer flow. Each can be used to focus management attention and indicate action before overall profitability has had time to decline to an unmanageable position.
2. Many controls depend upon the availability of data and it is here that many small retailers could improve. Systems such as EPOS offer great potential as costs of installation fall.

CHAPTER 11

*Accounting for the Smaller Retailer**

The Bolton Report of 1971 noted eight problem areas for small businesses. We shall focus on two of the most important, and continuing problems:

1. Raising and using finance.
2. Costing and control information.

A business needs finance which must be found from somewhere. Once 'found' it must be used efficiently and be documented as being used efficiently. The documenting of financial information provides a source to identify existing problems, anticipate future needs and 'account' to any relevant bodies as to the use of funds.

This chapter will cover these points more comprehensively under the following headings:

* The authors would like to acknowledge the help of Frank Cassidy in compiling this chapter.

1. The raising and use of finance.
2. Financial planning and control of the business.
3. The legal need for financial information.

To illustrate the large topic of accounting, the example of a butcher's shop will be used.

Raising and use of finance

Finance is needed when starting up in business and when expansion is necessary. However, to simplify exposition, the process of raising finance will be discussed from the point of view of a sole trader seeking funds from various sources in order to begin his business.

There are numerous grants and schemes available to the new starter such as the Business Expansion Scheme, and the Government Loan Guarantee Scheme, all offering incentives such as extended repayment terms,lower interest rates, and so on. Whatever source of finance is chosen, the attempt to raise finance will ideally start with a 'Business Plan'.

The business plan

This will consist of a detailed breakdown of the 'trader's' perception and apparent knowledge of the business areas being entered. It will show the products/services being offered, the market in which it will operate, the physical location, knowledge of competition and financial information. Invariably the financial side will include a budgeted monthly profit and loss account for anything up to three years, the expected sales revenue, and breakdown by type of sale, gross margin details, type of overheads to be incurred and very importantly, a detailed cash-flow statement. It is essential that the period between the inflow of cash through sales and the initial very high cash outflow is minimised.

So, if an entrepreneur were thinking of setting up as a butcher, then, first, he would need details of the type of premises to be used. Is he buying or renting? Secondly, his start-up equipment, the fixed assets of the business, the display cabinets, counters, the freezer, and so on, must be costed. All of these expensive items need to be financed before the first sale has been completed.

Next he will detail the nature of the business. One may think that 'selling meat is selling meat', and that the business plan will be sparse, but the butcher will have to show the potential financier why his business will succeed, and thus some detail is essential.

If the scenario were that he was setting up in a wealthy area, then immediately one can see that 'meat' is no longer just 'meat'. There are different cuts, types and qualities of meat. In a low income area the shopper will look for a value-for-money, economy-purchase joint of meat, that will last perhaps a few days. But in our butcher's area the populace will be able to afford better cuts and more exotic types of meat such as rump steak or veal, and thus his plan will reflect this target market. The area also affects his pricing decision because as he will probably sell a higher volume of steak, for example, he can probably live with a lower margin on such lines than in a less wealthy area. He may have researched the fact that people in his area do not enjoy eating meat without some sort of exotic flavouring, thus his projected sales may include various spices, garnishes and seasonings. So even with such a basic commodity as meat, a detailed sales analysis should be prepared.

The overheads to be included in his business plan would be similar to those of many other retailers, such as rent or rates, insurance, telephone, postage and advertising. However, an expense such as 'lighting and heating', which is basically electricity and gas, would be different as there would be a large amount of electricity required to keep shop displays cool, and, more importantly, run the freezer for his meat.

To summarise the business plan, the retailer is basically trying to forecast every eventuality that will have a bearing on his future business and hopefully 'sell' his idea to the provider of finance.

The correct type of finance

As stated earlier, there are numerous sources of finance, but the most important thing is to obtain the correct type of finance. Although an overdraft is relatively easy to acquire, and very flexible in terms of overdrawing only to the extent of the finance required, it is not suitable for purchasing long-term assets such as premises, or medium-term assets such as machinery. This is because an overdraft is short-term finance in that it can be readily recalled by the bank. Purchase of long-term assets should be financed by a long-term loan with fixed periodic repayment instalments.

Effective management of working capital (stock, debtors, creditors) can reduce the financing needs of a business. This would entail chasing up any debtors (not really applicable for a cash-sales-only retail business), not replacing stock (not very satisfactory if one is operating at an optimum stock level already), or more acceptable, living on credit (that is, attempting to gain an extended period in which to pay off one's trade creditors). This also needs to be carefully managed because if the credit period is constantly abused then suppliers will not supply. Many small businesses push their credit periods to the limit and operate on a 'Red Bill' basis with large creditors such as the gas and electricity boards, British Telecom and the local council. This means not paying the bills until the red 'Final Demand' invoice is issued.

For many retailers the ideal situation is to self finance from retained profits where the business is operating successfully and profits are made regularly. Of course, the proprietor must not withdraw all the profits from the business and must leave a residue to build up, which can be used to fund the future needs of the business.

To summarise, raising finance is not a difficult task in itself if a clear well-prepared plan is assembled which will appeal to the provider of finance. There are many sources of finance available to new businesses and businesses wishing to expand, but the crucial point is the need to match the type of finance with the use of that finance.

Financial planning and control of the business

Accurate and frequent financial planning is desirable so that the retailer can successfully monitor and direct the business. Larger companies would make use of a master budget, which basically comprises a budgeted profit and loss account, a balance sheet and cash-flow statements, broken down into smaller constituent parts such as sales and production budgets. The company would, at the end of a financial period, perform in-depth variance analysis to determine in which areas the actual figures differed from the budget, and try to discover why this occurred.

Rather than prepare an in-depth budget, a small retailer would be more likely to look at past performance and then direct future efforts to the areas that need attention. As a rough indicator the retailer may compare trading results for the year just ended, as shown in the profit and loss account, with the previous year's figures. This could be as set out in Table 11.1.

The butcher should consider and note the following points:

Margin analysis

The sales have doubled but the gross margin has fallen. Gross margin is given by the ratio of gross profit to sales and last year was 30 000/100 000 = 30 per cent. This year it is 50 000/200 000 = 25 per cent. There are many possible reasons for this. Selling prices may have been reduced in order to increase volume (if this was the plan

Table 11.1 T. Chop – butcher – profit and loss account

		This year (£)		Last year (£)
Sales		200 000		100 000
Cost of sales		150 000		70 000
Gross profit		50 000		30 000
Rates	1 000		1 000	
Wages	10 000		8 000	
Wrapping	1 000		500	
Rental of equipment	300	12 300	300	9 800
Net profit		37 700		20 200

then clearly it was successful). The sales mix may be different, that is, a lot more lower margin goods, in order to boost his volume. But the fact that sales have doubled in value terms would suggest something over and above a mere price-volume trade-off. It would suggest an external factor, perhaps something such as a well-established butcher down the road selling up, and not being replaced by someone else.

The retailer should investigate all of these areas and discover exactly why the figures have changed. With this knowledge the future strategy can be planned more effectively.

Cost analysis

Costs must be examined to see how they have changed in relation to this sales boom. An important point to note here is the distinction between fixed and variable costs, that is, the costs that do not change as volume changes and those that do change proportionately as output changes. Cost cannot always be easily categorised as fixed or variable, each situation must be studied individually.

If one looks at wages then both situations can exist where, for instance, someone is paid 'so much per unit' of the product sold/produced – this is a variable cost – or, as is normally the case, wages are fixed, where a set wage is paid regardless of output. Wages could also be semi-variable where a fixed wage is paid, but the worker is paid on a 'so much per unit' basis in addition, if certain targets are met – the normal situation where sales people are paid a bonus or commission. Employing part-timers and paying overtime could also be seen as a variable wage cost, extra help being taken on as and when turnover requires extra hours.

The butcher in the example would note that rates are a fixed cost, they are paid regardless of output. The wage figure is interesting. Although sales value has doubled, the wage figure has only increased by £2000. As we have no information to the contrary, let us assume that the sales have increased because of volume and not because of increased prices, and that the extra wage is due to overtime.

This would, rather belatedly, tell the butcher that his staff were perhaps overpaid previously in that only a very small amount of overtime hours were required to cope with the greatly increased output.

To help detect this problem in the future, the butcher could use two ratios which are very popular with the retail trade – 'wages as a proportion of sales' and 'sales per employee'. Using the former ratio one can see that 'last year' this worked out to be 8000/100 000 = 8 per cent, while this year it was only 10 000/200 000 = 5 per cent. As mentioned in chapter 10, both figures could be compared to those in similar businesses. The 'wrappings' figure seems more consistent with the increased sales, as this also has doubled.

On the face of it the rental of equipment would seem to be a fixed cost, but there may be an occasion where the equipment (say) electronic scales cannot cope with the increased volume, so another set of scales may be needed. (This is known as a stepped fixed cost in that the cost is fixed only for a certain 'relevant' range of activity.)

By looking in detail at his revenue and costs the retailer can plan his future business more effectively, and taking this a step further he can determine future volumes and prices necessary to 'break-even'.

Break-even analysis

To use a simplistic example – if one looks at a business problem facing the butcher which is how many decorated and garnished turkeys he needs to sell at £5 per turkey to cover the fixed costs of this project, in this case (say) £100.

The turkeys cost £3 each, and he pays a part-timer, skilled in the art, 75p per turkey to decorate and garnish the birds. The variable costs of the project are £3 + £0.75 = £3.75 per unit, and the difference between this and the sale price of £5 is £1.25, and this is the 'contribution per unit'. It is the contribution to the fixed costs and in this example we are trying to find the point where the contribution equals the fixed cost, this is known as the 'break-even' point:

$$\text{£1.25 (contribution per unit)} \times \text{break-even volume (BE)} = \text{£100}$$

Therefore,

$$\text{BE} = \frac{\text{£100}}{\text{£1.25}} = 80$$

Thus the butcher needs to sell 80 turkeys to break even on the project. Any volume over and above this figure will be profit.

This simple analysis can be used for all sorts of predictive information; for instance, if the butcher had a set volume, he could determine at what price he would need to sell to break even, or if he had a set price and volume, and cost of the turkeys, then he could determine the price that he could afford to pay his friend in order to break even. In reality it may be difficult for the retailer to gather together the information required for each variable in the puzzle, but rough estimates of the requisite figures could be used to give an approximate indicator to the retailer of the necessary approach.

Using ratios

Ratios were mentioned earlier and there are others available besides 'wages/sales' and 'sales/employee', which are useful for a retailer. Ratios such as the current ratio, the quick ratio, stock turnover and number of days credit received can all be valuable.

The current ratio, which is defined as current assets divided by current liabilities, shows the retailer how much cover he has got, if the current liabilities were suddenly recalled. Current assets would include debtors (not likely for a retailer), stock, and cash in hand and at bank. Current liabilities could comprise trade creditors and overdraft. Thus, if the retailer had stock of £1250 and bank and cash deposits of £750, and trade creditors of £2000 then the current ratio would be £750 plus £1250 divided by 2000 = 1. Therefore the retailer can be seen to *cover* his liabilities, that is, if they were recalled then he could convert his current assets quickly to cash if not already in this form, and pay off his short-term debts.

One may argue that stock is not readily convertible to cash and for this reason the 'quick' ratio may be a more accurate guide to how 'safe' the retailer is. This ratio is defined as current assets – stock divided by current liabilities, and in our previous example this would amount to 750 divided by 2000 = 0.375. Although the retailer's current liabilities are not completely covered, this is still a relatively healthy position, and a common one for the retail trade, in that a retailer will not usually have any debtors to include in his current assets figure.

The stockturn ratio, discussed in more detail in chapter 8, shows as a measure of how quickly the retailer is moving his stock.

The number of days credit received is a slightly more complex formula:

$$\text{If, } \frac{\text{Purchase for the year}}{365} = \text{(say) } \frac{\pounds 150\ 000}{365} = \pounds 411 \text{ purchased every day}$$

And, closing trade creditors = 33 000
Then, No. of days credit received = 33 000/411 = 80 days

Significant comment cannot really be made on any of these figures in absolute terms, because they only become meaningful when compared with other years, or other businesses in the same sector.

Cash-flow statement

One of the most important planning and control tools is the cash-flow statement. Because of the accounting principles and concepts which govern how accounts are prepared, it is possible to make a healthy profit yet still have a worrying overdraft at the bank. This can occur for various reasons but is basically due to two accounting principles known as 'accruals' and 'matching'. A profit and loss account is *not* prepared on the basis of cash received less cash spent equals profit. Instead expenditure is allocated to the time period to which it relates, and revenue is recognised when it is earned and not when the cash is received.

An example may explain things more simply. If we return to our butcher and assume that only the following three transactions have occurred (annual year end is 31 December):

1. In June the employers' liability insurance for a year was paid at £1000.
2. On 1 January a new refrigerator system costing £10 000 was purchased.
3. In December a bulk delivery of meat was made to an old people's home to be valued at £6000 (cost £2000 in November), and payment had not been received by the year end.

If we construct a profit and loss account under accounting principles using these figures only, then the transactions would appear in the profit and loss account thus:

The £1000 is for a year from June to June so six months of this is not in the current year. We allocate that part which relates to this year, thus 6/12 × £1000 = £500, which would appear as the insurance figure in the profit and loss account (no insurance for first 6 months).

When a large capital item such as the refrigerator system is purchased it is known as a fixed asset, and one must depreciate, that is, write off the cost using a method which reflects its loss of value. There are many depreciation methods but the most common is known as 'straight line' where one decides what the approximate age of the asset is, and then writes off the cost in equal yearly amounts. In this example if we decide that the asset would last five years, then the depreciation charge each year would be £10 000/5 = £2000, and this is the expense figure to appear in the profit and loss account.

The butcher, although not receiving payment for the meat sold to the old people's home by the year end, nevertheless has 'earned' the income from the transaction, in the current year, and we would therefore include the £6000 in his sales figure for the year.

If the profit and loss account were now to be constructed it would look as below:

		(£)
Sales		6 000
Cost of goods		2 000
Gross profit		4 000
Insurance	500	
Depreciation	2000	2 500
Net profit		1 500

A healthy profit has been achieved yet the bank balance would look disastrous. If we construct a very rudimentary cash-flow statement, this can be seen more clearly in Table 11.2.

This example (Table 11.2) although very simple and basic, serves to show why a cash-flow statement is imperative. A profit in the accounts of £1500 disguises a £13 000 overdraft balance at the bank.

As stated earlier, because of the accounting principles which govern the construction of profit and loss account and balance sheets, it is possible to lose sight of deteriorating liquidity. If the bank suddenly withdrew the credit facility then the retailer could be left without finance for his business and eventually would go under.

Many small retailers shy away from detailed planning and control of their business on the financial side and are quite content with their accountant's yearly or twice-yearly set of accounts prepared primarily for the tax man. But if the retailer can keep a day-to-day check on finances, then the business will be better controlled because key areas for attention can be identified.

As the cash-flow example showed, neglecting the financial side and depending solely on the year-end accounts to indicate whether a profit has been made or not, is a very inefficient way to operate a business. On the positive side, frequent cash-flow statements, ratio analysis and comparison checks may enable the retailer to realise that there is some spare cash to be used if an expansion or investment opportunity arose rather than reject it due to lack of knowledge of the true financial standing.

Table 11.2 Cash-flow statement

	Jan. (000s)	Feb. (000s)	March (000s)	April (000s)	May (000s)	June (000s)	July (000s)	Aug. (000s)	Sept. (000s)	Oct. (000s)	Nov. (000s)	Dec. (000s)	Jan. (000s)	Total (000s)
Balance B/F	–	(10)	(10)	(10)	(10)	(10)	(11)	(11)	(11)	(11)	(11)	(13)	(13)	–
Fixed asset	(10)													(10)
Insurance						(1)								(1)
Purchase											(2)			(2)
Receipt													6	6
Net (outflow)/ inflow in	(10)					(1)					(2)		6	(7)
Balance C/F	(10)	(10)	(10)	(10)	(10)	(11)	(11)	(11)	(11)	(11)	(13)	(13)	(7)	

The legal need for financial information

The only reason many small retailers will have accounts prepared is to satisfy the taxman and the Vatman. If it were not for this requisite many would trust their instincts to tell them if business was 'good' or 'bad'. Leaving aside the business reasons why records should be kept, as discussed in the previous section, let us now look at the legal reasons for keeping them.

A salaried worker pays income tax on his earnings usually through the PAYE system. The self-employed businessman cannot do this, thus he must detail his earnings, less his expenses, in order that the Inspector of Taxes can decide what tax he must pay, and this statement usually takes the form of a profit and loss account. To use our butcher again as the example – he would probably take a bag of financial information into his accountant at the year-end. This would comprise a cash book, details of takings, bank statements, cheque stubs, paying-in book, invoices paid in the year, any unpaid invoices at the year-end, and note how much stock there is. From this, and using the accounting principles mentioned earlier, the accountant will draw up a set of accounts which will include a profit and loss account and balance sheet, perhaps something similar to that in Tables 11.3 and 11.4.

There are many terms used in these accounts which may be unfamiliar to the reader, but which are common accounting parlance.

Table 11.3 T. Chop – butcher – profit and loss account for the year ended 31 December 1989

Sales		100 000
Cost of sales		60 000
Gross profit		40 000
Slaughter and haulage costs	15 000	
Wrapping and consumables	2 000	
Repairs and renewals	500	
Business insurance	300	
Telephone	150	
Rates	450	
Wages	5 600	
Sundry expense	150	
Accountancy charge	350	
Bank charges	80	
Motor expenses	400	
Depreciation	500	
Light and heat	600	
Posting, stationery, advertising	250	26 330
Net profit		13 670

Table 11.4 T. Chop – balance sheet as at 31 December 1989

Fixed assets			
	Cost	*Accumulated depreciation*	*Net book value*
Refrigerator	1 200	300	900
Fixtures & fittings	2 500	600	1 900
Premises	18 000	–	18 000
Butcher's equipment	400	20	380
			21 180
Current assets			
Stock	2 500		
Cash at bank	1 200		
VAT repayable	850		
Prepayments	250	4 800	
Current liabilities			
Trade creditors	(2 500)	(2 500)	
Net current assets			2 300
Net assets			18 880
Financed by			
Opening proprietor's capital		14 300	
Add: Profit for Year		13 670	
		27 970	
Less: Proprietors private drawings		9 090	
			18 880

An in-depth discussion of net current assets, net assets, and so on, can be found elsewhere.[1]

When these accounts are received at the Inland Revenue Office, the Inspector will scrutinise certain key areas such as the gross margin, and these will be compared with previous years. Any small deviation will have to be explained, as in a 'cash only' business there is a great temptation to underdeclare the takings figure and thus ultimately understate the tax liability, which will be reflected in a lower margin.

The Inspector will also look at the repairs figure to ensure that no capital items, that is, those that should be noted as fixed assets on the balance sheet have been included. This is because a capital item only gets a percentage of its cost allowed for tax yet true repair costs are in the profit and loss account and are wholly allowable for tax purposes, therefore the temptation again is to include some capital items in the repairs figure.

The taxman will also endeavour to check that the butcher has not included private expenses, that is, non-business expense in the profit and loss account. Thus he may question the retailer closely about such things as motor expenses to see that only the business portion was included, and not any private mileage.

When the profit figure is settled then the butcher will pay income tax on this figure, less personal allowances, in the same way as the salaried worker, except that the latter will account for his liability by the administratively more convenient method of PAYE.

Value Added Tax

Accounting for VAT is another bane of any businessman. It will not be discussed in any detail here except to note that at the time of writing one is liable to output tax at 15 per cent on standard rated taxable supplies and can claim input VAT at 15 per cent on standard rated supplies received. The net difference between the output and input, is either payable or claimable at the end of the VAT period. There are also zero-rated and exempt supplies and a host of various rules about registration, deregistration, and so on. All of these can be studied in free leaflets provided by the Customs and Excise detailing the numerous intricacies. One should note, however, that because of the difficulties in determining the output tax on sales in a cash-only business, there are a number of retail schemes available which simplify the record-keeping problem for VAT purposes in these business.

One such retail scheme is detailed here.

Scheme C

Any retailer with a VAT trade classification from 8201–8239 which includes grocers, bakers, fishmongers, butchers, and so on, can use this scheme. Other requirements of the scheme are that the taxable turnover must not be over £75 000 p.a. and goods can be supplied at both standard and zero rate, although the scheme cannot be used if services are supplied or for goods that are grown or made by the retailer.

The scheme is simple enough to operate. The retailer adds up the cost including VAT of the standard rated goods received for resale in the tax period. The fixed mark-up of these goods is added on. Then the VAT fraction (currently 3/23) is applied to this and this will be the output tax due. For example:

Cost of goods received in the period (including VAT) –	£1 000
mark-up (@ 20%)	200
VAT *inclusive* selling price	£1 200

Apply VAT fraction (3/23)

$$3/23 \times 1200 = £156.52 = \text{output tax}$$
$$3/23 \times 1000 = £130.43 = \text{input tax.}$$

VAT payable by the retailer is output tax − input tax = £156.52 less the VAT in the purchase price, £130.43, that is £26.09.

The reason for these retail schemes is that in a cash-only business it would be very difficult to calculate output tax on each sale. These schemes developed basically to enable retailers to use known information (that is, cost of goods received) and to work out the VAT figure from this.

To summarise, accounts are necessarily prepared for small businessmen to enable HM Inspector of Taxes and HM Customs and Excise to assess the businessman's tax liability. A cash-flow statement *should* also be prepared in order to help the retailer monitor his business, discovering the areas which need his attention, to enable him to focus on his strengths and reduce his weaknesses in the future.

Keypoint summary

1. Accounting and finance covers a large area, thus any chapter on the subject can only hope to skim the surface of as many different facets of the subject as possible. Much of what has been noted here in relation to a small retailer applies equally to a large conglomerate. The same basic lessons must be learned.
2. The two vital watchwords for the small retailer are planning and control. It is not satisfactory to be content with a cursory glance at the year-end accounts to solve the retailer's financial conscience. A keen eye must be kept on day-to-day operations, using the control methods outlined earlier, such as ratios, break-even analysis, cash flows. The results can be used to develop the future potential of his business by means of sound and detailed financial planning.
3. The independent retailer, operating as a sole trader, is likely to be involved in paying two taxes, VAT and income tax. If the business is incorporated the retailer will pay VAT and corporation tax, plus income tax on any salary or dividends taken out of the business.
4. The small retail business must look to meeting the two issues of raising finance and control through a clear analysis and prediction of the finances of the business.

CHAPTER 12

The Future of the Smaller Retailer

The message for small retailers

Few retail commentators disagree about the future of the multiple operators: continued expansion leading to a larger share of the retail market place; success to be achieved through improved efficiency with EPOS computer systems; the development of new retail concepts starting from the exploration of 'niche markets' and the provision of new 'out-of-town' leisure-orientated shopping centres.[1] The concern of this book, however, has been the position of the smaller retail operator within the retail environment. There is no broad consensus of opinion about their detailed future. Some observers using statistics of declining market shares and dramatic falls in outlet numbers may have entitled this final chapter the 'demise' of the independent! At this stage in the book, however, the reader will be aware that the authors take a more optimistic view of their future.

The small retailers do have, and will continue to have, an important role to play within the retail market-place. Not only will they continue to provide goods and services that large multiples either cannot or do not want to offer the customer,[2] but they will always add a 'crucial ingredient to the quality of life and the social balance'[3] in any community in which they happen to be located.

The main message throughout the book has been to encourage small retailers not to try to compete directly with the multiples on price, but to find alternative methods of differentiating themselves and survive in the competitive retail environment. Guidance has also been given on how to develop a competitive advantage by offering a good service to customers (whether by long opening hours or well-trained staff), by selecting an appropriate location, or developing a specialist product offer. Faced with increasing polarisation within the retail sector as a whole, smaller retailers need to continue to devise distinctive formats for their business (for example, through franchising or adopting the convenience trading philosophy). No small business should shy away from new technology available to retailers. Small store bar-code scanning systems are already on the market with associated software packages providing full purchasing and inventory control. Electronic shelf price display units are currently being developed by the multiples and will soon be available to the small-scale operator. Although the multiples may take the lead in technological innovation, small retailers should be aware of all developments and be prepared to adapt the most appropriate features to their individual retail operation.

The authors accept that not all small retail shopowners want their business to grow to the size of Marks and Spencer or Kwik Fit. One of the objectives of the book, however, has been to emphasise the idea that, whatever the size of operation, businesses should be operated in the most cost-efficient way. Also important is the idea that every owner/manager should be aware of, and be able to respond to, the opportunities and threats facing his/her particular business. Chapter 2 gave a detailed SWOT (strengths, weaknesses, opportunities and threats) analysis of the small retail sector, but the emphasis in this final chapter will be on the opportunities available in the future for the independent retailer, beginning with some predictions about consumer spending patterns to the year 2000, and how these will affect the small retailer and concluding with a more detailed look at two key development areas – franchising and convenience retailing.

Responding to consumer needs

It has been stressed that the survival of any retail operation depends on the business being able to respond to the needs of its customers. So what will retail customers want in the year 2000, and what products and services will they require an independent to provide?

The first question has been addressed by a number of retail commentators and several characteristics have emerged about the 'consumer in the future'. First, consumers will be relatively *wealthy* and, although prosperity may not be shared equally, any poverty will be relative rather than absolute. Consumers will have extra money to spend on their homes, cars, clothing and hobbies. Leisure interests will be very important to the consumer of the future as 'work' becomes less of a priority. Another characteristic has been referred to as *'individualism'*. The idea that the family, once taken to mean parents, children and grandparents, and so on, will become a less important feature of society as the family made up of one or two individuals take its place. One writer[4] feels change in the family structure will lead to the dominance of a consumer MAFIA (middle-aged, independent and active) in the market for consumer goods and services. The mafia will consist of couples who may have had one or two children in their late 20s, and by 40 will have a car plus a home and will be ready to spend on a 'hedonistic' lifestyle. The majority of consumers are likely to be *'mobile'*, implying not only ownership of one or two cars, but also well 'travelled', taking holidays not just in Europe, but in more exotic parts of the world like Japan and India. Wider experiences will ultimately be reflected in demand for foreign goods (particularly food) specifically associated with one region of the world.

This overall picture of the consumer of the future ties in with the more detailed demand prospects broken down by product sector in government economic trend statistics. Recreational activities have been identified as an important growth area within total consumer spending. This area contains durable spending on radios and hi-fi equipment which is expected to increase by the year 2000 to account for nearly 50 per cent of total recreational spending. Dramatic increases are also anticipated for sports goods, toys, records, tapes and films, and so on. The importance of holidays to consumers of the future is emphasised by estimates of rapid growth in spending on air travel. Spending on bus and coach travel is expected to decline.

In the *food* sector, the general trend in spending on healthy products – bread, fruit, vegetables, low calorie lines – is set to continue with a corresponding decline in sales of meat, milk and other dairy products. In the *drinks* market the rapid increase in popularity of soft drinks is likely to continue, as is spending on alcoholic drinks. An increase of about 3 per cent per annum is predicted until 1990, with a further increase stimulated by the extended licencing hours and the EEC legislation removing excise duties from alcohol. However, just as public pressure groups have been largely responsible for the demise of the cigarette and tobacco market, anti-alcohol lobbies are predicted to have a greater impact on the drinks industry in the future. A ban on alcohol advertising is already anticipated to bring the UK in line with other countries within the European community.

Finally, in the *clothing sector* spending on women's and children's clothing is projected to account for 60 per cent of the total clothing market by the year 2000 as the relative importance of menswear and footwear declines. In absolute terms, however, healthy growth is expected in these sectors too.

In most areas care needs be taken when assessing the share of UK consumer spending which will filter back into the UK retail sector. It is anticipated that many areas, particularly travel and communication, will be adversely affected by the influx of European competition brought about by the relaxation of the trade barriers within the EEC.

Relevance of market information for smaller retailers

There are a number of reasons why the above information is important for the independent retailer. First, and perhaps most obviously, no matter how efficient or prosperous a business may be in the short term, long-term survival depends on operating in growth markets. Some product sectors identified above show better growth potential than others, and smaller retailers need to frequently renew their product portfolios to ensure they are featuring these ranges. For example, from a broad sector perspective travel agents and sport/leisure stores look to be well placed for the future, and products like canned drinks, convenience foods (particularly in the frozen and chilled sectors) and ethnic and foreign dishes need to be prominently featured.

Secondly, because small business owners are often so involved in the day-to-day running of the shop, they forget to consider the store in relation to the wider retail market-place. Consequently, not only do some businesses lack an overall sense of direction, but many small retailers miss opportunities to exploit the strengths of their operation in other areas of the market. Continuous market research is often more valuable to a smaller retailer than a multiple because of the fact that the business can respond more quickly to any changes highlighted. Large companies are often criticised for undertaking *ad hoc* market research, that is, only looking at trends in consumer spending and demographic statistics on a one-off basis when they are about to launch a new product or open a new store. The same criticism can be applied to smaller firms. Many owner/managers collect information when they are about to set up in business but fail to carry out research on a continuous basis. Most areas have a library, university or polytechnic which can give small firms reports and information on special sectors of retailing. One garden centre retailer had recently been invited to a European gardening exhibition in Cologne. Although he was keen to explore opportunities for importing new products, his knowledge of the German horticultural market was virtually non-existent. He visited the library and information unit of a nearly university and found three reports focusing specifically on this market. The preparation paid off at the exhibition.

Although an awareness of changing consumer demands in any market is essential to success, the other side of the equation involves being able to meet these demands in a cost-effective manner. Retailers are increasingly turning to franchising as a form of operation enabling them to keep overheads at a minimum, and at the same time operate a business with a clearly defined and developed image.

Franchising

Franchising is a marketing-orientated method of distribution in which one person grants a license or franchise to another person, the franchisee, which permits the franchisee to use the franchisor's trade name, trade marks and business system in return for an initial payment and further regular payments.[5] Some of the more famous franchise operators include Circle K (UK) Ltd (convenience retailers), Budget Rent-a-Car International (the car, van and truck rental service), Bally Grove (UK) Ltd (shoe retailer), Don Miller (hot bread kitchens), Kentucky Fried Chicken (GB) Ltd (fastfood). Of the 88 franchisors registered with the British Franchise Association as at July 1988, over 60 per cent had operations which fall within the authors' definition of retailing.

Although a form of franchising has been evident in the licensed trade with public houses on a tenancy basis for many years, the present format appears to have been originated in the US after the Civil War by the Singer Sewing Machine Company, who were looking for a method of distributing their products. There was rapid growth in franchising in the USA in the 1960s and 1970s, and at least one-third of all retail sales are presently carried out by this method, with nearly 2000 companies offering franchise opportunities. Although growth may have been initially slower in the UK, a survey in 1987 indicated that there were already 25 000 franchised businesses employing over 175 000 people. Popularity of retail franchises is expected to continue to grow. Mr Desmond Cooke, chairman of the British Franchise Association, predicted in a *Guardian* article that by 1991 there would be a gross turnover in franchising of more than £9 billion.

The Appendix to this chapter outlines a number of advantages and disadvantages of franchising for a smaller retailer. Once again the most important consideration when assessing the long-term potential of a franchise business is the characteristics of the market it is in. Is it a growth market? How many competitors are there? Is there a clearly segmented target market? The computer hardware and software and video hire markets for example, both initially proved to be inappropriate for franchised operations because of the peculiar characteristics of the markets. The best view of the success of franchising as a mode of operation for a smaller retailer must logically come from franchisors or franchisees who have well-established businesses.

One of the most well-known retail franchise operations is Tie Rack Ltd, retailers of neck wear and accessories. Tie Rack began franchising in 1982, and by 1988 had over 199 franchised shops. At the annual Convention of the British Franchise Association early in 1988, Andrew Rankin told delegates about the secrets behind Tie Rack's success. He identified three reasons why Tie Rack has been able to expand as a franchise operation – first, because there was not as much capital required to expand in this business format as in traditional forms of retailing. Secondly, because responsibility for the everyday running of a store could be left in the hands of competent, well-trained franchisees, leaving more time to concentrate on the strategic problems of the business. Third, and most importantly, however, Mr Rankin felt that success was due to the fact that Tie Rack franchisees were so highly motivated towards their businesses. Franchisees felt that Tie Rack shops belonged to them in every sense of the word and were more motivated to make more sales and ultimately, therefore, increased profits.

As Mr Rankin stressed 'every business relies heavily on its human resources – even more so in the retail trade which involves a high degree of interaction with the public'. He emphasised the value of training, stressed in chapter 9, stating that franchisees all attended an in-depth two-week course prior to a unit opening, as well as regular updating sessions.

Mr Rankin's comments echo the authors' own views as to the suitability of franchising for a small retailer. Not only are small retailers flexible enough to cope with any new trading format, but such owners/managers normally display the personality characteristics so important for success: the enthusiasm for retailing as a profession; a capacity for hard work; but, most importantly, a genuine interest in people whether customers or staff. Franchising offers two options for the smaller business. For the person who wants a lower risk opportunity of running their own business, purchasing a franchise is attractive. The successful small retailer, who has pioneered a new sector, can look to expand more easily through franchising.

Convenience retailing

Another trading identity which might be considered viable for the future survival of the independent grocer is convenience trading. Although the first UK 'convenience' stores was set up by a UK company, the concept of convenience trading was inherited from retail experiences in the United States. As mentioned in chapter 1, although precise definitions differ, the 'convenience' store is usually regarded as the equivalent of the general or village store designed to serve a well-defined and located geographical location offering 'top-up' products and extended trading hours. The format is in line with the so called Momma and Poppa stores in the USA. There are about 2500 stores which might be defined as convenience stores. Case Study D describes the development and success of one such store.

For ease of analysis the 'convenience' market can be broken down into four discreet subgroups:[6]

1. *Special convenience stores*. Outlets most like the original American model. Ownership is both American (7-Eleven and Circle K) and UK (Europa). Circle K is claimed to be the chain set for the most rapid expansion in the 1990s following its purchase of Sperrings in 1987, with 120 outlets presently and 500 anticipated by 1992.
2. *Traditional grocery/wholesale-based convenience stores*. These form the bulk of the outlets and are made up of wholesale symbol groups such as SPAR and VG. Although still grocery based, the number of traditional lines has been reduced. Own-label products play a particularly important role in these outlets, for example, Happy Shopper, My Mum, etc.
3. *CTNs* (*Confectioners, tobacconists and newsagents*) who have been forced to diversify away from their traditional product base of cigarettes, sweets and tobacco into grocery lines.
4. *Petrol stations and forecourts* have used the fact that they have suitable sites with good customer traffic and are able to open long hours. The relatively low margins on petrol have encouraged them to diversify into other product categories including grocery lines.

A number of factors have been identified to explain the growth of 'convenience' retailing. First, the obvious existence of a market for the 'convenience' package in working men and women who find it difficult to shop during normal hours, as well as the elderly or unemployed who prefer to buy smaller quantities of goods more frequently. 'Convenience' also relates to proximity to consumers' homes. A recent survey on convenience stores estimated that 80 per cent of shoppers actually walk to the outlets.[7] Their sites have largely become available in local shopping centres due to the closure of smaller branches of the big grocery retailing groups.

Some commentators have noted how these 'advantages' are gradually being eroded by the multiples with the substantial increase in their opening hours and the switch in emphasis to convenience products. It is predicted that some 500 supermarkets will be retailing magazines and newspapers by 1989.[8]

Although there may well be developments which slow down the growth of convenience stores, most writers believe that convenience trading is still an area to be exploited by the smaller operators. The sector is predicted to be worth £2bn by the end of the decade.[9] However one defines 'convenience' retailers in the future, it is the philosophy of trading which the smaller retailer might find useful to adopt: the emphasis on convenience products forces the smaller retailer to rationalise his range, limiting the depth or variety as discussed in chapter 6. The needs of the target market have been clearly identified for the retailer, and although detailed preferences may vary (for example, some providing fast foods or video hire facilities), every aspect of the store can be organised to meet these needs.

Every piece of statistical evidence available on the future of retailing indicates that independents will continue to lose market share to the multiples over the next 20 years and the number of outlets will continue to fall. These statistics cannot be totally ignored. The authors' view, however, is that the statistics do not reflect the true nature of the independent sector. Since existing classifications do not take into account the different forms of trading operation in which small retailers presently take part, it is safe to say that insufficient small businesses are included in the government definition of retailing. Our view is that smaller retailers will survive for the reasons identified at the beginning of this chapter, but may, in fact, must emerge under the guise of a different trading format as they continue to respond to changing customer needs and preferences. The key to success lies in the flexibility the small retailer has to respond quickly to these changes. A small corner-shop selling mainstream grocery products today has the flexibility to become a franchised dry cleaning and repair service in the space of a few months. We are able to predict with some confidence that while the independent sector may continue to lose market share for some years, there are areas in the retail market that cannot be adequately served by a multiple format. Some point of equilibrium will be reached where the scale economies of the multiple will be balanced by the flexibility of the independent. As the wealth of the nation grows so will the opportunities. While the independent sector may continue to lose its market share of mainstream retailing, the value of the independent sector to the economy and to the owner/operator will remain.

Appendix to Chapter 12

Advantages and disadvantages of franchising for the independent retailer

Advantages

1. Benefits of bulk purchasing and negotiating power of franchisor.
2. Lack of management expertise overcome by training given by franchisor.
3. Unrestricted use of franchisor's trade marks, copyrights/patents, and so on.
4. Benefit of continuous Research and Development, access to market information on new technology, products, and so on.
5. Benefit of national 'image' of franchisor.
6. Usually less capital required to set up than if going alone.
7. Clearly defined 'target market' and geographical market towards which to structure business.
8. Owner business benefits including assistance with site selection, preparation of site, purchase of equipment, stock, and so on.

Disadvantages

1. Relationship imposes regulations and controls on quality standards.
2. Tendency to become overdependent on franchisor. Expectation of day-to-day involvement.
3. Payment of initial franchise fee and continuing sums.
4. Business vulnerable to policy mistakes by franchisor. Innovations may be inappropriate to franchisee.
5. Franchisors' policies may affect profitability of franchisee. Franchisors' priority equals high turnover (from which continuing franchise fee obtained) versus franchisee emphasis on profitability.

Help for the Independent Retailer

Some useful addresses

Alliance of Independent Retailers
Newton Road
Worcestershire
0905–28165

British Retailers Association
Commonwealth House
1/19 New Oxford Street
London WC1A 1PA
01–404 0955

National Association of Shopkeepers
Lynch House
91 Mansfield Road
Nottingham NG1 3FN
0602–475046

Independent Footwear Retailers Association
New Ash Green
Dartford
Kent DA3 8QY
0474–874704

National Federation of Retail Newsagents
Yeoman House
Selforde Street
London EC1R OHD
01–253 4255

British Franchise Association
Franchise Chambers
75a Bell Street
Henley-on-Thames
Oxon RG9 2BD
0491–578049

Institute of Grocery Distribution
Letchmore Heath
Watford
Herts WD2 8DQ
0927–67141

Retail Consortium
Commonwealth House
1/19 New Oxford Street
London WC1A 1PA
01–404 4622

CASE STUDY A
*The Rangill Store**

Background history and development to 1988

Mr Bhati took over a 21-year-old leasehold property in 1975. A small retail outlet situated between Central and Churchwood North tube stations at 11B Spring Gardens, Richmond. Prior to 1975 the shop had been run by an elderly gentleman, Mr Jameson, who had kept it as a small delicatessen. Mr Bhati took over and revised the product range to include fresh bread, milk, vegetables, home-made sandwiches, hardware items and frozen food. The shop also retailed a range of speciality canned and packet goods including Indian curries made by his wife Surinder. Sales escalated between 1975 and 1978 largely, according to Mr Bhati, due to the store's location and varied product range. From 1978 to 1988 there was no marked year-on-year improvement in sales despite an off-licence being added in 1980.

Location

The Rangill Store was situated about one mile from Central Shopping Centre and Churchwood High Street on the corner of a side street. Figure 1 (CS.A) outlines in more detail the surrounding area.

The famous Central lane Eye hospital was situated within twenty minutes' walk. A one-way traffic system was in operation outside the store but Mr Bhati did not see this as an obstruction to customer flow. He commented 'It is certainly much easier for customers to park near my shop than in Churchwood High Street'. Gloucester road itself stretched for about one mile and was made up of large Victorian terraced houses, some so dilapidated that they appeared unfit to live in, yet many in the process of being renovated for wealthy property developers. Others were already occupied and decorated in traditional 'Duchess of Duke Street' style as one occupant remarked. Some of

* This case study is based on a number of similar businesses. It has been prepared to illustrate some general points and does not reflect or represent the situation in any one business.

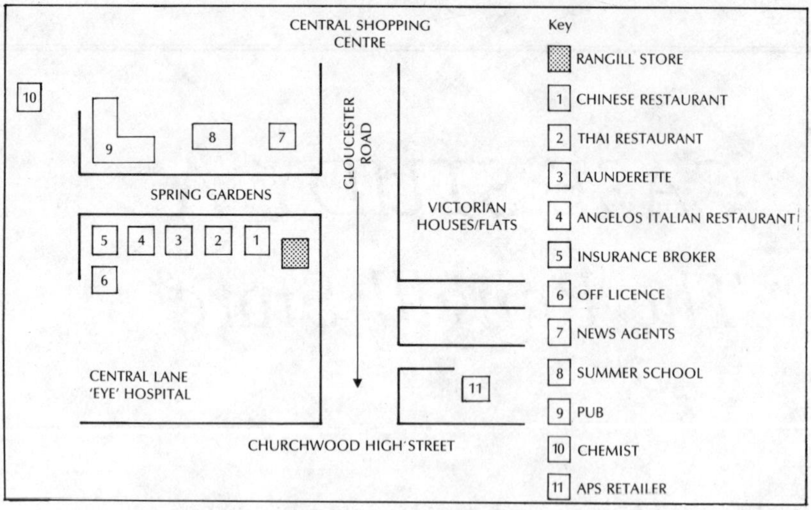

Figure 1 (CS.A) Location of Rangill Store

the houses had been converted into bed and breakfast accommodation and housed some of the 'DHSS families' who were waiting for the council to provide them with permanent homes. As with many areas of London, there were severe housing and labour shortages. A small flat in one of the terraced properties would cost a minimum of £120 000 (some twelve times average earnings). A local employment agency quoted £4 per hour as the minimum rate for unskilled labour. Bar staff, shopworkers and cleaners could expect to earn at least £4.50 in other areas of Richmond.

The shop itself was run by Mr Bhati and his wife Surinder. They travelled to work by car every day from their home in Greenwood. They had a 13-year-old daughter, and a son who, in 1988, had just taken his 'A' levels. A place at university studying economics and engineering awaited him if he obtained the necessary grades. The family were Sikhs and attended the local Gudwara at least twice a week. Mr Bhatis's religious beliefs prevented him from selling cigarettes in the store even though he admitted 'customers ask for them every day'. Surinder was asked to work longer hours than she would like due to the problem of obtaining reliable staff in the area. She explained:

> The money is not a problem. My husband would be quite happy to pay the going rate for a good, hardworking, honest worker. We did have a good person last year who stayed for 8 years, and we paid almost £3! Unfortunately the employee left to take up a similar position closer to home. He was a Sikh too, but his wife did not like him working until 8 o'clock every night.

The shop was open 9.30 a.m. until 8.00 p.m. Monday to Saturday. On Sundays the store opened later at 11.30 a.m. and closed at 6.00 p.m. Mr Bhati commented on the importance of Sunday as a trading day. 'My takings are very similar to any other day and that is with 4 hours less trading. Saturday is obviously our busy day. We usually take 20 per cent more on a Saturday than any other day'. Mr Bhati admitted that the hours were very long and the work very difficult. 'My wife has a bad leg and really should spend more time at home. It is a difficulty during the holidays when our daughter is not at school. I like to try to get home at lunchtime to see her'. Their daughter was preparing for a holiday in Yorkshire at a religious school where she would be taught the more complex elements of the Sikh religion. Mr Bhati had not had a holiday for 13 years. The only other staff used since the store opened consisted of a retired gentleman who came once a week to clean the shop. He had become ill six months earlier but sent his grandson in his place. Christian, originally from Holland, he was studying English at the local school but had agreed to work for Mr Bhati in his holidays and weekends and some evenings. Mr Bhati could not let him serve behind the counter because he could not yet understand English, but he let him stack the shelves and help him unload some of the heavier deliveries.

Competitors

Presto had taken over the Co-op in the Central shopping centre two years earlier. As Presto opened six days a week as opposed to the Co-op's 4½ days, and one hour later in the evening, they had certainly had an impact on Mr Bhati's trade. The nearest competitor, however, stocking a similar product range to Mr Bhati was situated in Adlington Road. The store was affiliated to the local APS wholesale group and sold most known value items (KVIs) at the same price as Mr Bhati. The store had chosen to adapt a clear APS identity with posters and display material both inside and outside the store. Although the Adlington Road store had once had a delicatessen counter, it had proved unsuccessful and was replaced by larger refrigerated units with packaged cold meats and cheese. Prepacked sandwiches were also on sale although retailed at 10 pence more than Mr Bhati's freshly-made varieties. Although the owners were also Asians, they did sell cigarettes and had an off-licence section. Mr Bhati's real competitor for alcohol sales was the off-licence at the end of Spring Gardens. Two of the adjacent restaurants allowed guests to bring their own wine and Mr Bhati admitted that the alcohol sales reached a peak between 6.00 p.m. and 8.00 p.m. 'We could do a lot more if we were open later but there is the off-licence down the road. People don't seem to notice it!' Like cigarettes, Mr Bhati had little interest in the drinks section.

Customer profile

Following the advice of a business acquaintance, Mr Bhati had carried out a survey over a two-day period to try to identify the characteristics of his customers. Table 1 (CS.A) outlines the results of a few hours of the survey. Although he knew quite a lot of information from standing behind the counter for 13 years, the survey did highlight some interesting points. A high percentage of foreign students came into the store during the period from the School of English on the opposite corner of Spring Gardens. Mr Bhati was also proud of the number of TV celebrities who called for their 'top-up' items of shopping. There was a TV studio nearby which produced documentaries and children's programmes. Members of the cast often spent time in Mr Bhati's store chatting to Surinder about their work.

Table 1(CS.A) Results of customer survey
Day:– Tuesday; Time 10.00am to 4.00pm

Time	*Sex*	*Ethnic*	*Purchase*
10.00	M	E	Bread, fruit juice, peaches
	M	E	Milk, honey
	M	E	Large coke, bread
	F	E	Potatoes, margarine
	M	E	Milk, 2 cartons
	M	S	Unsliced bread, milk
	F	E	Lucozade, confectionery
	F	A	Tuna, soap powder, bread, mayonnaise
	F	Sp	Sandwiches, continental cheese
	F	As	Biscuits
	F	E	Orange juice, confectionery
	M	S	Sweets, lemonade
	M	S	Sweets, coke
	F	Sp	Soap powder, ice creams (2)
11.00	F	E	Bottled Perrier water
	F	E	Coke, spring onions
	F	WI	Indian incense, round cake
	F	E	Sliced bread (2)
	M	E	Apple pie slice and Coke can
	F	E	Ribena
	M	Sp	Tomatoes, cabbage, banana
	F	E	Washing Powder
	M	E	Paint, screwdriver, knife, etc
	M	E	Kitkat, biscuits, foil
	M	E	Bananas

Time	*Sex*	*Ethnic*	*Purchase*
1.00	M	E	Crisps, sweets
	M	E	Crisps, sweets, can of pop
	M	Ir	Cheese sandwich, pie
	M	E	4 bottles cider
	M	Ir	Sandwiches, milk, pot noodle, crisps, roll
	M	E	Sandwiches, milk
	Party order		50 samosas/savoury snacks
	F	E	Coke, margarine
	F	E	Ryvita, crisps, nectarine
	M	E	Alpen, milk
	F	WI	Milk (14)
	F	E	Coke, ice cream
	F	E	Tomato, onion, spaghetti, parmesan cheese
	F	E	Sandwiches(3)
	F	Fr	Sandwiches
	M	E	Frozen curry, samosa
	F	E	Pork pie, crisps
	M	E	Crisps, sandwiches, chocolate
	F	Ch	Lucozade, sandwiches
	F	E	Milk, bread, butter
2.00	F	Ir	Large bottle of Lilt
	F	Ch	Chewing gum, milk, bread
	M	E	Bells whiskey, can of Coke
	F	E	Ice cream

	F	E	Coke, bread, salami sausage
	F	E	Fresh bread, bananas, Kitkat
	F	E	1/2 bottle champagne, 1/2 bottle Bells whiskey
	M	Ch	Fresh orange juice
12.00	M	E	Batteries
	F	E	Bananas, tomatoes, Perrier water, Flora, peaches
	M	Ch	Coke
	F	Ch	Fruit juice
	M	E	Bottled Perrier water, Gouda cheese, small biscuits
	M	E	Milk
	M	E	Mars, can of pop, extra strong mints
	Restaurant employee		Fresh juice, extra strong mints
	M	E	Sandwiches, milk
	M	Fr	Cheese, german sausage, crusty bread
	M	A	Sandwiches, milk
	F	Fr	Croissants, milk, fruit juice
	F	As	Sweets, box of biscuits
	M	Ir	4 cans of Coke, petrol
	F	Ir	4 cans of American beer, soap powder
	M	E	Onions, cucumber, nectarines
	F	Ir	10 cans Harp lager, 4 crisps, samosa
3.00	M	E	Ryvita, salami sausage, vodka, diet Coke
	M	E	Lucozade (4), can 7UP, Coke
	F	Sp	Ice creams (2)
	M	E	Lettuce, tomato
	F	E	Pies, cans of pop, crisps, cold meat, sandwiches
	M	E	Luxury pizza, gouda cheese, croissants, milk, brie
	M	E	Perrier water
	F	E	Shortbreads, yoghurt
	M	E	Sausage rolls, 2 pts milk, fruit juice (carton)
	M	E	Bread, margarine, lucozade
	F	Fr	Croissants, cheese
	F	Fr	Sandwiches, yoghurt

Note: 1. Mr Bhati had to supervise other areas of the shop while carrying out the survey, therefore each hour only captures a percentage of the total customers.

2. More than 50% of the customers visited the store every day.

Key: Ethnic

Fr – French
Sp – Spanish
Ir – Irish
A – American
S – Scottish
WI – West Indian
Ch – Chinese
As – Asian
E – English

Customers called in from the three restaurants adjacent to the shop. A lot of their customers preferred to eat early, usually straight after work. Mr Bhati put this down to the high cost of getting in and out of the city. Angelos, the Italian restaurant appeared every year in the Egon Ronay Good Food Guide. The manager of Angelos had a 'slate' for regular orders with Mr Bhati. He would send a member of staff to the store about ten times every day for necessities and speciality lines. He took 30 fresh french breadsticks every morning and also bought cooking foil, pieces of fruit and cheeses or cooking oil for use in the restaurant.

Freshly-made sandwiches sold well between 11 a.m. and 2 p.m. when the carpenters and bricklayers renovating the adjacent terraced houses took their lunchbreak. They rarely just bought one packet, however, and usually asked for pies and sausage rolls which were heated in Surinder's microwave for a modest charge. Because Mr Bhati was anxious that he was seen to treat his customers fairly, he insisted that Surinder placed two signs in the shop informing people of the extra 15 per cent he put on the price of pies for heating them up. Workmen also bought Mars Bars, crisps, packets of apple pies and cakes to supplement their sandwiches, as well as a few cans of beer. A popular new line, which Mr Bhati had taken from a passing salesman was 'Mars Bar' flavoured milk. The workman found it very good value for money at 30p and substituted it for their usual pint. The success of the product, however, did not help Mr Bhati's already complicated pattern of deliveries. The Mars representative only called once every six weeks and Marshall dairy, who delivered the standard milk lines, did not have plans to list the product in the near future.

The store also received frequent visits from customers of the launderette, usually for change for the machines, but sometimes for sweets to 'keep the children quiet'. They also bought small quantities of soap powder for when the launderette dispenser ran out.

Product range and layout

Although Mr Bhati was aware that he needed to get rid of some of the product lines in the store, he was very concerned that he shouldn't let any of his customers down by not having the particular variety they wanted. 'I don't want someone to come into the shop to buy something they bought a few months ago and be disappointed', he commented. His policy was to give the widest possible choice to appeal to every income group. Simply by walking around the store, wiping the dust off the cans, and counting the number of brands of each commodity, any observer could see the operational problems caused by having too wide and deep a range.

The range of soups stocked highlighted Mr Bhati's dilemma. One shelf displayed 14 varieties of 14 oz Heinz soups, and 3 varieties of Heinz large special soups, 2 varieties of Heinz wholesoup, 2 weightwatchers and 10 varieties of small tins. Baxters and Campbells were also featured with 12 varieties of 14 oz Baxters large soups and 2 varieties of speciality Scampi and Lobster Bisque. Fifteen varieties of Baxters were stocked including both condensed and ordinary quality range. He had 20 tins of Campbells main course on display too. Two other speciality brands were on display – turtle and Brandy and Gourmet chicken and herb. The latter Mr Bhati claimed he had bought when on special offer at the cash and carry.

The layout of the store did not facilitate good stock control. As soon as deliveries were received they were stored at the top of the warehouse steps which were located at the front of the store. The fresh fruit and vegetables delivered daily were also displayed at the front of the store, but often looked untidy and dirty due to the dust and fumes which swept in from the road through the open door. A small stand carrying a very limited range of videos was situated opposite the fruit and vegetables. Two freezer cabinets 'made up the first aisle' in the shop. Although much of the freezer stock was bought in from Blakemores frozen foods every month, Surinder had introduced a number of authentic Indian dishes into the range including home-made curries and naan breads. A battered notice appeared above the range which read 'real Indian curries, we will leave it to your taste to try them!'. The frozen food cabinets also displayed cans of babyfood and other baby products like nappies and baby bottles on top. Opposite was a range of 'stationery' including pens, pads of paper, sellotape, freezer bags, childrens' books and toys. Mr Bhati was loath to take out any of the non-food range because of the 'high margin'. 'I make 50 per cent on most of these things he commented, that is stationery, light bulbs, wallpapers and paint'. On most other items he claimed that about 25 per cent was average, but 'he wasn't exactly sure'. He stocked a wide range of household cleaning items like soap powders, scourers and polish – usually the well-known brands like Pledge and Vim. 'We sell a lot of these in the summer when they are cleaning out the flats to rent to tourists', commented Mr Bhati. Brushes and dusters lay next to the provisions fridge which was always overflowing with milk; skimmed/semi-skimmed, flavoured as well as ordinary pasteurised. Milk retailed at 25p, the same price as all the other stores in the area. Customers came into the shop specifically for milk but frequently bought other items like speciality cheese or yoghurt from the same fridge. The yoghurt display almost filled another of the cold units. However, on close inspection many revealed out-of-date cartons. Surinder loved yoghurt and used about six cartons a day either in cooking or simply eating from the fridge. The out-of-date problem occurred mainly with cottage cheese and lines of margarine and butter.

Drinks were displayed separately in the shop. Alcoholic drinks were displayed behind the tills and a fridge containing soft and alcoholic drinks was situated at the other end of the store. Fruit juices such as Ribena, orange, grapefruit and so on were stacked next to the confectionary stand. Mr Bhati allowed the Mars representative to 'merchandise' the confectionary stand when he visited as he had been impressed by the 'shelf layout' plan he was working to. Blakemores who supplied the bulk of Mr Bhati's Frozen Foods had given Mr Bhati an ideal layout plan for his frozen food section based on takings in other small retail outlets, but Mr Bhati had been too busy to study it, let alone implement it. Although Mr Bhati was aware of different ideas about display, he felt that most of his customers were regulars and knew where everything was in the store already. As long as they could find things he was not concerned about tidiness or aesthetic appeal.

Products were obtained from a variety of different sources. He calculated that he spent about £1150 per week at Bestways Cash and Carry. He used his own van to collect the merchandise on a Monday morning every week which left Surinder overseeing the shop. He also had a regular delivery from APS on a Tuesday at the same time. Although he only spent about £100 per week, they delivered the goods and he was able to order one week in advance from the price list order form (P.L.O.F.). This gave details of bonus offers available

Table 2(CS.A) APS PLOF (week 24)

Delivery Week Commencing 11.8.88

Bin. no.	*APS price(£)*	*Cost food product description*	*Packing (Qty × Size)*	*Retail price (£) Unit*	*Care*	*Retail profit on return*
030 120	2.59	APS Premium liver	12 × 390g	0.31	3.72	19.93
030 121	2.59	APS Premium Pork	12 × 390g	0.31	3.72	19.93
030 122	2.59	APS Premium Beef	12 × 390g	0.31	3.72	19.93
030 123	2.66	Choosy Salmon	12 × large	0.30	3.60	15.03
030 124	2.66	Choosy Beef	12 × large	0.30	3.60	15.03
030 125	2.66	Choosy Rabbit	12 × large	0.30	3.60	15.03
030 126	2.66	Choosy Liver	12 × large	0.30	3.60	15.03
030 127	3.33	Felix Beef	12 × large	0.37	4.44	13.75
030 128	3.33	Felix Chicken	12 × large	0.37	4.44	13.75
030 129	2.82	Go Cat Gourmet Beef	12 × 185g	0.32	3.84	15.55
030 130	2.82	Go Cat Gourmet Fish	12 × 185g	0.32	3.84	15.55

and recommended retail prices at which to sell the goods as well as the profit made on each item. Table 2 (CS.A) gives an extract from a PLOF.

Although the delivery service was convenient for Mr Bhati, he found the range of products available to be rather limited. He had wondered whether to obtain the majority of his lines from APS and stop going to the cash and carry, but was unsure how to assess the cost effectiveness of the proposal. To maintain a varied product range, Mr Bhati obtained the rest of his goods from a number of sources outlined in Table 3 (CS.A). As he had no formal system for recording stock levels or detail product sales on a regular basis (other than the annual stocktake and the cash in the tills at the end of each day), he used his purchase figures to give some indication of sales. He received four deliveries of fruit and vegetables each week, but admitted that many of the tomatoes and bananas went 'off' and had to be either reduced and sold off or thrown away. His priority when purchasing goods was the price, and he admitted he found it difficult to resist a good bargain offer at the Cash and Carry. Several of the display ends in the shop had dump bins full of 'special offer' goods. They seemed to remain for quite some time and tended to make the shop look even more cluttered and jumbled up.

The second most important consideration was the amount of credit available from the supplier. Peak Farms, for example, did not expect payment for six weeks, APS, however, restricted it to two weeks after invoice. Mr Bhati had no formal way of assessing the value of credit. Goods were priced as Mr Bhati felt appropriate. Sometimes if deliveries were piling up Surinder simply looked at the price on the cash and carry pack, divided by the number of tins or packets and added a few pence extra. Mr Bhati referred to three sources to get price information. First *Shaw's Guide to Fair Retail Prices* published monthly and obtained from the cash and carry. This contained lists of selling prices for almost all branded merchandise. Secondly, *The Grocer Price Index*, again published every month, with *The Grocer* magazine, and finally the PLOF issued by APS.

Mr Bhati's accounting system was primitive. The old till at the counter had two keys which had to be pressed after every item according to whether the

Table 3 (CS.A) Major sources of supply

Supplier	*Product supplied*	*£ pw*	*Deliveries*
Marshall Dairy	Milk	170	daily
Helios Bakery	Bread (Greek)	65	daily
Sunlight	Bread products	60	daily
My Mother	Bread products	45	daily
Evergreen Brothers	Cash & Carry (general)	400	weekly (use own van)
Blakemore	Frozen food	100	weekly
Peak Farms	Ham, bacon	50	weekly
Plush Port	Eggs	35	weekly
Petty Wood	Japanese food	32	weekly
Harwood Farm	Fruit and vegetables	180	daily
Rebinski	Sausage		weekly
Thompsons	Cheese, yoghurt	45	weekly
Atlantic Harvest	Cheese, gammon	25	weekly
Losely	Ice-cream	24	weekly
Nut House	Speciality nuts	12	weekly
La France	Croissants, French bread	12	daily
Zorba Delicassies	Speciality cheese	10	weekly
Barkers' hardware	Hardware items	17	monthly
APS	General	900	weekly
Bestways Cash and Carry	General	1150	weekly (own van)

item bore VAT or not. The sole purpose of this was to help Mr Bhati fill in the VAT forms in the evening. An annual stocktake took place in the store, and an accountant friend of the family prepared his books for the taxman. Mr Bhati was unable to say precisely how much stock he had on the premises at any one time, but he worked on the assumption that he needed to have at least a full 'pack' of every item in the stockroom at any time, as well as countershelf stock, for example, 12 packets of granulated sugar on the shelf and a pack of 12 or 24 in the stockroom downstairs.

Promotion

Where appropriate, Mr Bhati used the posters and display material offered by APS. Surinder used a black pen and card to produce her own labels. There was no room for a window display as deliveries, always overspilt into the window and blocked customers' vision. Mr Bhati had recently considered using carrier bags as a method of promoting the business. He had paid £40 to have a design put on one bag with the 'RANGILL STORE' printed in bold letters but was loath to spend 3 pence per bag to get any more printed. The whole issue of carrier bags was a little confusing. Presently he obtained some from APS for 2p per bag and charged customers 6p. Some had complained and Mr Bhati was unsure whether it would be better for business if he let the customer have them free.

The future

Mr Bhati realised that his business was only performing in line with inflation. It seemed that initially he had been able to exploit the trading advantage associated with the store location but this was no longer sufficient and he realised that there must be weaknesses in the rest of the operation. There were so many things he felt he could do but it was a question of deciding priorities.

CASE STUDY B

*The Happy Nut House**

Being made redundant from your father's printing firm is not the best start to a commercial career but that was the situation for Michael Dunn in Liverpool in 1972. He joined a local health food shop as its manager until the shop was bought by a large chain, Holland and Barrett, in 1974. Dunn moved on to become an area manager with a smaller chain, Country Life Wholefoods, and left them in 1976, this time with the objective of starting his own health food retail business.

With £200 in the bank and an overdraft facility of £2000 secured on his house, he opened his first shop in Aintree, Liverpool.

His company's name was Hillstart, reflecting Dunn's interest in cycling, the choice of store name, the Happy Nut House, was as distinctive as the yellow and brown facia that became the company's hallmark in later years.

In 1977 a second store was added in the centre of Liverpool. Soon after Dunn made the acquaintance of the Shone brothers, who had previously managed a family milling company. The Shones wanted Dunn to act as a consultant in the wholesaling of milled products. Dunn declined their offer but returned to them with the idea of buying out his old employers, Country Life Wholefoods, each party holding 50 per cent of the equity of the expanded business. The idea appealed and the owners of Country Life eventually agreed a price in 1979. Apart from closing the relatively distant Northampton shop which was sold, eight outlets were converted to the Happy Nut House name. Over the next eight years new shops were added in Rhyl, Northwich, Bolton, Sheffield, Southport, Fulwood and Buxton. Health-foods had become big business in Britain and Dunn believed the market had

* This case study was prepared by Professor Gary Davies of Manchester Polytechnic. It is designed to provide the basis for discussion of the issues facing the smaller retail chain.

shifted away from the dowdy backstreet store into the mainstream of High Street retailing.

The health food market

Concern about a healthy diet had grown rapidly in the latter half of the twentieth century. In the 1950s the emphasis had been on 'proper' meals. In the 1960s dieting to keep slim became fashionable. In the 1970s lack of dietary fibre and a propensity to consume too much sugar, salt and hard fats were being blamed for a wide range of health problems from heart disease to varicose veins. In the 1980s artificial colourants and additives became the targets of both nutritionists and the popular press alike.

The greater publicity given to dietary issues was having its effect on consumption patterns. Sales of wholewheat or wholemeal bread tripled between 1981 and 1984. Consumption of fresh fruit and vegetables was on the increase while sales of full cream milk and meat were falling. Farmers were looking more and more to organically-grown crops, and over two million of Britain's population by 1987 were said to have embraced vegetarianism wholly or in part.

Within this environment sales of health foods were booming, while total food sales remained somewhat flat. Market research company Mintel predicted a 75 per cent increase in the health food market from 1982 to 1986.

The market for health foods was divided between a number of distinct sectors with the specialist stores estimated to hold the largest single slice in 1984. This sector was however, largely fragmented with a predominance of small, family-run stores. The total number of specialist stores was estimated at 1700 in 1987.

The single largest chain, Holland and Barrett, with 160 stores, contained a number of franchises and was part of the large Booker McConnell group of companies. The same group included Brewhurst Wholesale, a distributor of health foods who supplied an estimated 60 per cent of the total market including 83 per cent of Holland and Barrett products and other associated interests including Allinsons and Prewitts. The next largest chain was Lifecycle, based solely in the South of England. A voluntary association of independents, Realfare, had attracted some 550 members. The Happy Nut House with 17 retail outlets located in the north-west of England were the third largest chain by 1987.

The typical healthfood shop carried a varied range of products other than food – such as vitamins and dietary supplements. Gross margins on many lines were relatively high at around 27 to 33 per cent, compared, that is, to the margins expected by most mainstream food retailers for packaged groceries. Some independents trading in a typical 450- to 800-square-foot store might achieve £8000 per week turnover, although others might be only marginally profitable and offer their owners more satisfaction in retailing health food products than in financial returns.

Other types of retail outlets had competed traditionally for some of the same market as the healthfood shop. Vitamin products, for example, were well within the territory of the chemist. More recently the changing attitudes among the public to what they were eating had attracted the attentions of the food multiples.

In 1986 Marks and Spencer launched a range of low calorie, low salt, sugar and fat meals which were free from artificial additives and preservatives.

Safeway and others had moved to sell organically-grown vegetables and fruit. Tesco had evolved an approach to nutritional labelling of their own label foodstuffs that was to be copied by the manufacturers of national brands.

Certain products that had only ten years earlier been seen as unusual or even faddish had become major sellers for the multiples. Muesli was a typical example. By 1987 only 15 per cent of muesli was sold through healthfood shops. Other products such as bottled spring water became difficult to offer at a reasonable price if you were an independent, given the purchasing power and discount policies of the food multiple.

Less well-known products such as lecithin, carob and mung beans were still the preserve of the specialist healthfood store which could offer advice to the uninitiated. However, only some 20 per cent of High Street shoppers had ventured into a healthfood store. Many regarded them as cranky and overpriced.

The health food buyer

Various sources offered somewhat different views of the typical healthfood shopper. One source identified the main purchasing group as almost exclusively female, middle aged, and of socio-economic group C1. Another identified two groups, one young, professional and living in the south-east, the other much older and less regionally concentrated. A third source (D'Arcy, Masius, Benton and Bowles (1986) 'Healthy Eating Study') identified six groupings in the population by their different attitudes to health foods and diet. These included the 'practising lentilist' who was into aerobics and who imposed her bran-led diet on her family. These 'superfits' as they were called tended to be below middle age, affluent and living in the south. Another older group, defined as the 'older concerned' were adapting to new tastes partly in response to media pressure but with the practical motive that 'death was a concentrator of the mind and appetite'. While there was some overlap between the various types of classification, it was clear that generalisations about the healthfood customer might be less than useful in guiding the promotion of products and outlets. Added to the general market were the special interest groups such as vegetarians (who accounted for some 15 per cent of purchases) and others such as body-builders and diabetics who were purchasers of specific specialist products. Finally, herbal and homoeopathic remedies provided another and a major source of revenue for the healthfood shop from those who sought an alternative to the National Health Service.

Happy Nut House

By 1987 the Happy Nut House (HNH) traded from 17 stores as detailed in Table 1 (CS.B). Various stores had been substantially refitted or relocated from first opening. The growth over ten years to a turnover of over £3 million had been impressive and Michael Dunn was planning to make further increases in the size of the business.

HNH made considerable use of market research. In 1981 a survey identified their typical shopper and consumer as female who visited twice a week to spend between £2 and £4. HNH staff were considered friendly and informative 'when they had time to be'. The major reason given for shopping

Table 1 (CS.B) Happy Nut House Stores 1987

Branch	*Square footage*	*Opening date refit/resite*
Aintree (Liverpool)	210	1976
Birkenhead	750	1979/80
Bolton	700	1983
Burton on Trent	662	1979/84
Buxton	650	1987
Chesterfield	900	1979/81/86
Liverpool Whitechapel	210	1976
Manchester Deansgate	1000	1979/83/85
Northwich	476	1981
Rhyl	900	1986
Rochdale	446	1981
Salford	750	1981/86
Sheffield	700	1984/86
Southport	600	1986
Stockport	650	1979
St Helens	800	1979/81/85
Warrington	800	1979/85

at HNH was that it was the only outlet for the goods required. HNH had received some criticism summed up as being 'tatty – amateurish' with the shops being described as 'crowded'.

In 1983 the company had assessed the result of an experimental television advertising campaign on Granada. Unaided recall of the Happy Nut House name had been 20 per cent. This had fallen in 1984 by 4 per cent to 16 per cent, leading to the view that some form of continuous promotion might be beneficial.

Data was gathered regularly on customer-flow rates (measured by number of transactions) for each store. Table 2 (CS.B) shows a typical week's measure in February 1987 and the average expenditure per visit for the same week. Shops with a hot food takeaway such as Chesterfield and Manchester Deansgate tended to have the higher customer flows but lower expenditure per visit figures.

An analysis of the 13 stores owned by HNH in 1986 and retained in 1987 showed that the total number of customer visits had declined by 4.4 per cent while expenditure per visit had risen by 5.7 per cent.

Ordering of products was the responsibility of individual stores who kept a manual record of each product line on a stock card. An analysis of all product lines based on three stores over a four-week period in 1987 based on these cards is shown in Table 3 (CS.B). No central records were kept of sales by individual product line. Some 13 per cent of the company's relatively large range were own label.

Gross profit margins varied enormously on individual products, from 20 per cent for bread to 47 per cent for vitamins. Margins on own label tended to be higher, and selling prices lower, than on manufacturers' brands. HNH prices and for own label in particular, certainly did not appear to compare unfavourably with those in rival healthfood shops. However, as Table 4 (CS. B) reveals, the larger multiples covered many traditionally health food store lines at lower prices.

Table 2 (CS.B) *Customer flow and customer expenditure per store (with rank order). Wage costs as percentage of turnover*

	Customer flow	*Average spend (£)*	*Wage cost (%)*
Chesterfield	4 595	1.66 (12)	11.3
Manchester Deansgate	4 559	1.66 (11)	11.8
Sheffield	4 479	1.35 (17)	12.0
Stockport	3 739	1.98 (3)	11.2
Warrington	3 212	1.67 (8)	10.9
Liverpool Whitechapel	2 869	1.77 (6)	11.0
Bolton	2 468	1.66 (9)	13.0
St. Helens	2 354	1.48 (16)	12.0
Burton on Trent	2 283	1.66 (10)	12.8
Birkenhead	1 982	2.06 (1)	12.9
Salford	1 859	1.68 (7)	14.4
Rhyl	1 606	1.64 (13)	12.2
Buxton	1 486	1.63 (14)	15.0
Rochdale	1 454	1.82 (4)	12.0
Southport	1 121	1.51 (15)	19.3
Northwich	869	1.80 (5)	16.4
Aintree	667	2.04 (2)	14.8

Table 3 (CS.B) *Product range analysis*

Product category	*No. of lines*	*% of Turnover*	*No. of own-label lines*	*Typical % of total footage*
Beverages	74	3.4	–	4.3
Biscuits	45	1.9	–	3.4
Bread	19	1.5	14	1.8
Breakfast foods	70	2.9	23	8.4
Cosmetics	165	3.6	–	6.0
Dairy	75	3.1	3	2.4
Dried fruit & nuts	60	4.5	54	3.2
Flour	19	0.6	7	1.3
Frozen foods	30	–	–	–
Herbal remedies	274	24.7	–	11.4
Herbs and spices	53	0.6	53	3.0
Honey and jam	83	4.5	4	4.5
Juices	31	1.6	–	2.6
Oils and vinegars	21	1.0	1	0.9
Pulses	26	0.8	26	0.9
Sandwiches	13	1.1	13	0.3
Slimming	31	4.1	3	2.0
Snacks	128	4.4	–	10.2
Sports supplements	88	7.0	–	5.5
Takeaway	73	4.5	–	1.7
Vegetarian	221	5.7	6	8.9
Vitamins	142	15.9	15	7.6
Other	6	2.7	2	9.1
Total	1747	100.0	228	100.0

Table 4 (CS.B) Selling prices of the same or similar products in various outlets (pence)

Product	Asda	Sainsbury	Tesco	Superdrug	Boots	HNH
Orange Juice 1 Litre Pack	45	42	45	42	–	54
Bran (500g)	37	38	–	39	–	38
Cafe Hag (100g)	178	178	178	188	188	199
Wholemeal Flour	51	–	54	–	–	63
Perrier Water	53	47	–	49	–	59
Jordans Health Bar (multipack)	–	75	75	69	62	78
Honey (llb) own label	–	62	69	69	–	79
Lecithin Granules	–	–	–	–	255	255
Ginseng	–	–	–	–	447	469
Vecon (large)	–	–	–	–	159	159
Multivitamins (30) own label	–	125	125	50	–	119

Table 5 (CS.B) HNH top-selling own-label lines

1.	llb clear honey
2.	Peanut butter
3.	Lecithin
4.	Whole cashews
5.	Prunes
6.	2lb clear honey
7.	llb set honey
8.	Cod liver oil capsules (250)
9.	Cod liver oil capsules (100)
10.	Brazil nuts

Own-label products offered HNH protection from the larger multiples in two ways. First, direct price comparison was more difficult for the consumer than on branded items and secondly, HNH's own image could command a premium. The price disadvantage of 10p or more in Table 4 (CS.B) on own-label honey did not stop the line being HNH's top-selling own-label line. Table 5 (CS.B) lists HNH's ten top-selling own-label products in 1987.

HNH conducted further market research in 1987 on people leaving their stores. Some 84 per cent of a sample of 150 had made a purchase. Of the 25 people in the sample who had not made a purchase, six claimed to have been put off by price and seven because the product sought was not in stock.

The 'walkout rate' (as it is sometimes called) of 16 per cent who had entered the shop but left without buying compared well with figures of 50 per cent for department stores in general, 30 per cent for Marks and Spencer in particular, but much lower figures for high street food retailers.

When asked about the HNH own-label range, many respondents to the survey commented favourably, but over a third did not realise that the

Table 6(CS.B) Abstract of market survey results 1987

Male shoppers	33%
Female shoppers	67%
Social class ABC1	40%
C2	32%
DE	28%
Age 16–24	23%
25–34	22%
35–44	20%
45–54	12%
55+	23%
Came from home	79%
Came from work	17%
Other	4%

Most respondents had travelled less than 5 miles
32% did not eat red meat
52% had no children
36% of shoppers were Social Class B (Managerial/Professional) aged less than 44.

company had its own range. When asked about competition, 18 per cent visited branches of the leading healthfood chain, Holland and Barrett, 25 per cent healthfood shops, 17 per cent Boots or Superdrug for healthfoods and only 6 per cent a supermarket.

More evidence on the HNH customer came from a survey conducted by a student who had approached the company to undertake a market research project as part of her course. She conducted interviews at six store locations on 180 HNH shoppers in total. Table 6 (CS.B) presents some of her data. It conflicted in only one way with HNH data in that she identified a much higher rate of visit to Boots and Superdrug, which could have been due to the use of the words health product rather than healthfood in the questionnaire.

Employees

In 1986 HNH employed 104 people including only 8 males. Their average age was 32. A substantial number, more than half, were part time, working normally 10 to 15 hours a week. The typical store would have five employees, two or three being full time. (Wage costs amounted to some 12.5 per cent of turnover, a major cost area.)

The company organisation is shown in Figure 1 (CS.B). Michael Dunn, in addition to the normal responsibilities of a managing director, looked after site acquisition. Wendy Davison's role as product controller was a new one. She was responsible for all product matters, from purchasing to merchandising, including promotion. Previously she had been an area manager and had been responsible for the introduction of takeaway food. Carole Kitchen and Barbara Rollett each had their own specialist roles apart from seeing to stores

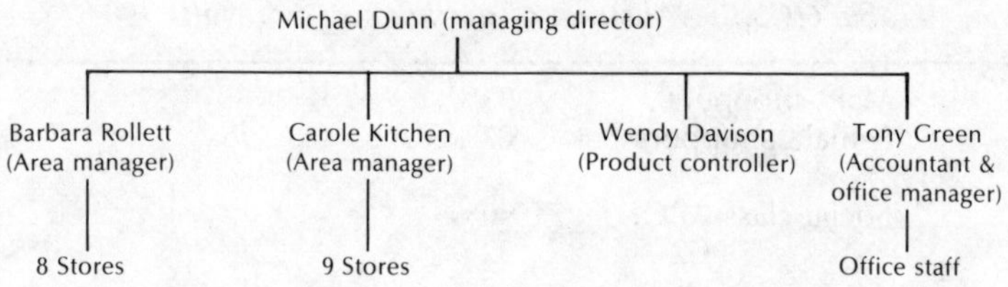

Figure 1 (CS.B) Organisation chart 1987

in their areas. Carole Kitchen had a special responsibility for personnel and Barbara Rollett for some promotional activity.

An examination of labour costs by Carole Kitchen, conducted with a view to making greater use of part-time staff, had concluded that any financial advantage would be outweighed by the lack of commitment and high turnover rate found in part-timers. Turnover was nearly four times higher in HNH among part-timers than among full-timers.

Turnover of full-timers was also an issue, especially among trainee managers, due to the high cost of training. It took around a year to train a manager and 60 per cent left or were dismissed during this period.

The company retained an external training consultant for much of their training which was normally conducted in the training room above the Warrington store. Systematic shop-floor training was being introduced in 1988 in Customer Care and Product Knowledge.

Promotion

HNH had experimented over the years with a number of promotional ideas, including a series of television adverts in 1983 which had had no measurable effect on turnover. Recall of the company name after the campaign had been reasonably high and had fallen slightly the following year in the absence of such advertising.

By 1987 HNH was not spending any money on above-the-line promotion. Instead they had been running a competition where the winner was given a holiday in the USA. A number of instore promotions were also linked to specific products. An annual sale where prices were reduced across the board seemed to increase volume offtake, but by moving expenditure forward as regular customers stocked up and took advantage of the lower prices rather than buying more in total.

Inside the store leaflets were available on various products and window stickers and window displays were used to promote individual lines. All healthfood shops had to be very careful as to what claims were associated with herbal remedies, vitamins and homoeopathic medicines. Many of these products could be regarded as coming within the scope of the various pieces of legislation on medicinal products which required stringent testing for safety and efficacy. Such legislation had not been widely applied to the kind of products found in a healthfood store.

The external store design and internal fixtures could be regarded as a major form of promotion for any retailer. The Happy Nut House name was a striking one and the company logo stood out on the high street. The logo had a subscript of 'the home of healthy living' (which also appeared on the company's letter headings, for example) emphasising the presence of other than healthfoods in the company's offer.

Managing the business

Table 7 (CS.B) shows some of the main control statistics used by Michael Dunn to track the progress of his business. A number of factors impinged upon HNH profitability. Of all the company's costs, rents and rates had risen the fastest. Rent reviews on the exclusively leasehold properties could increase costs by substantial amounts overnight. In the company's financial years 1983 to 1985 there had been only five rent reviews. In 1986 there had been six. Rent and rates had risen 48.5 per cent per square foot over the four years while sales per square foot had risen only 22 per cent. Some of the newer stores were large and occupied prime sites. Sales growth in these stores had been somewhat lower than expected.

Table 7(CS.B) HNH statistics

Year to	*June '83*	*June '84*	*June '85*	*June '86*
Sales (000£)	1 813	2 117	2 440	3 076
No. of stores	14	14	15	16
Total sq. feet	7 709	8 599	9 515	10 741
Sales per sq. foot	235	246	256	186
Rent & rates per sq. foot (£)	16.9	21.3	22.3	25.1
Rent & rates as a % of sales	7.2	8.6	8.7	8.8
Customers (000)	1 344	1 533	1 652	1 928
Average customer spend (pence)	135	138	147	159
Employees	85	86	84	104
Hours worked	117 364	120 134	118 638	123 841
Sales per hr worked (£)	15.5	17.6	20.6	24.8

The number of customers entering HNH stores between 1983 and 1986 had risen 43 per cent but this was due mainly to the increase in the number of shops. If the customer-flow increase was measured per square foot, it had risen only 3 per cent. The average expenditure per visit had risen 18 per cent to £1.59 by 1986. However, this was still very low compared to most food businesses and most other types of retailing.

Gross margins were holding up well but HNH were under pressure on many branded items from the larger multiples. The increasing overhead burden on the company led to a small trading loss in the 1987 financial year.

The company management undertook a comprehensive review of all aspects of the business which produced much of the data contained in the

Table 8(CS.B) Ideas produced by the management review

1. Increase selling prices.
2. Increase number of own label lines.
3. Examine new opportunities including a takeaway healthfood store and an outlet selling just nuts.
4. Consider centralised purchasing.
5. Reduce labour costs by using more part-time employees.
6. Advertise in local press, radio or TV.
7. Improve shop-assistant training on selling techniques.
8. Introduce Electronic Points of Sale [EPOS].
9. Centralise merchandising.
10. Experiment with different merchandising approaches, displaying main selling lines at aisle ends.
11. Increase product range by examining products such as organically-grown vegetables.
12. Rationalise product range by reducing product variants and eliminating slower lines.

tables and figures in this case study. Table 8 (CS.B) lists 12 of the ideas produced for further evaluation.

The major issue facing HNH was how to retain the product specialism that had been the basis for their business and how to offer the customer better service and, in particular, advice, without that same customer then deciding to buy from the cheaper multiples.

CASE STUDY C

*Marketing Four Leisure Centres**

By 1985 a shorter working week, earlier retirement and greater affluence amongst those in work had all led to a substained growth in leisure time and in the ability to pay for the goods and services with which to enjoy it. Somewhat in contrast, unemployment had risen to unprecedented levels, offering millions plenty of time, if not the disposable income, to enjoy their unsought opportunity for leisure activities.

The leisure market was large and diverse ranging from theatres to funfairs, from the single most popular activity of watching television to a whole range of sporting activities. The sports market itself could be subdivided in a number of ways: team sports and individual sports; sports participants and sports watchers; 'dry' sports and water sports; sports involving high physical activity and those involving comparatively little effort.

Apart from the general trend towards more leisure activities, sporting activities had benefited from changing attitudes to health which seemed to have sent a whole generation onto the streets in jogging gear. Organisations catering for the sports sector of the leisure market included sportswear manufacturers, magazine publishers and providers of sports facilities. The last mentioned group divided into two main groups, the private- and publically-funded sectors.

Public funding of sports and leisure facilities had a long history. Most swimming baths had been constructed using public money and were operated at a deficit as a public service. In recent decades the trend had been away from the construction of 'public baths' and towards the building of leisure

* This case study is intended to illustrate the issues involved in marketing four publically-owned leisure centres. It has been prepared for discussion by Professor Gary Davies of Manchester Polytechnic.

centres catering for a variety of sports, including swimming, and also other leisure activities. A swimming pool was still a main feature but the typical centre contained a multipurpose sports hall, squash courts and related facilities including a bar, cafeteria and outdoor courts.

Many leisure centres had been constructed in the 1960s and 1970s by local authorities using borrowed finance. Repayments of capital and interest charges were met by increasing the local taxes (rates) paid by householders and businesses and by virtually automatic increases in money from central government in rate support grant.

The Conservative Government in power in 1985 had tightened central government's grip on local authority spending and, as a matter of policy, had been limiting its own contributions to rate support while at the same time discouraging local authorities from meeting any resultant shortfall in expenditure by increasing rates. Most local and county councils had acquiesced to government policy. The exceptions, for example, Liverpool City Council, made the national headlines.

There was therefore growing pressure on councils to examine all their budget areas to seek economies. Some services, such as refuse collection, had been privatised by individual authorities.

Most areas in Britain came under two local authorities, a local Borough Council and a County Council. Leisure centres were the responsibility in the main of Borough Councils, although County Councils could contribute financially where the centres were used by schools during school hours, schools being funded by County Councils.

Many leisure centres were built adjoining high school premises. These 'joint-use' centres were usually not open to the public during school hours. Broadly speaking, the running costs during school hours were borne by the County Council. Out of school hours, that is, in the evenings, at weekends and during the holidays, the costs were borne by the Borough Council.

Nationally few, if any, leisure centres made a profit, particularly if capital costs and any depreciation were allocated to them. Borough Councils met the shortfall between revenue and expenditure (which included an allowance for rates) out of their rate and rate support incomes.

Local Authorities were run in Britain by full-time staff. All council employees reported to a management hierarchy in the same way as in any large organisation, with the difference that key areas of activity were monitored by elected members of the community. The elected councillors represented the interests of their local ratepayers and, generally, also represented one of the national political parties.

Councillors voted on key issues on party as well as on local interest lines. Each major area of expenditure by a council tended to have a subcommittee of the full council with some delegated authority to oversee it.

Macclesfield leisure centres

The Borough of Macclesfield formed part of the County of Cheshire in north-west England. Its northern boundary was with the County of Greater Manchester (disbanded in 1986, and reverted to individual local authority units). The more northerly centres of population in the borough – Poynton, Wilmslow, Knutsford, Bollington and Alderley Edge, were home to many who commuted each day to work in the City of Manchester.

Table 1(CS.C) Population statistics (1981 Census)

Major towns/villages	*Population*
Alderley Edge	4 228
Bollington	6 930
Knutsford	13 675
Macclesfield (town)	46 832
Wilmslow	30 207
Bucklow	9 236
Disley	4 413
Macclesfield (rural)	33 482
	149 003
Macclesfield and Bollington	67 290
Wilmslow and Alderley Edge	37 991
Knutsford	22 911
Poynton and Disley	20 811
	149 003

The largest centre, Macclesfield, lying in the middle of the borough, had its own commerce and industry. It had been a centre for the silk industry but was by 1985 less involved with silk and had evolved a broad business base.

The population of the borough in the 1981 Census was 149 003 spread over 200 square miles, much of which was semi-rural land. Table 1 (CS.C) shows the 1981 census data on the major towns and villages, and Figure 1 (CS.C) a sketch map of the borough. Also indicated are the locations of the five leisure centres in the borough. Bollington leisure centre was not part of the borough's responsibilities, being a locally funded initiative.

The Poynton and Knutsford leisure centres were 'joint-use' facilities in that they were attached to the local state high schools. Wilmslow and Macclesfield centres were situated near to schools but were not funded as joint-use centres although they derived considerable income from local state and private schools.

Knutsford Centre

Knutsford had the oldest of the four leisure centres. It had a 110 × 80 ft sports hall (large enough for six badminton courts); two squash courts, a 25 × 9m swimming pool; a cafeteria and bar. Of the two other main rooms, one was used mainly for keep fit and marshall arts and the other as a multi-gym. In 1985 a new solarium had been opened next to the multi-gym. The centre also had the use of four outside tennis courts.

Poynton Centre

Poynton was the second of the joint-use sites with a sports hall the same size as that of Knutsford, four squash courts (one of which had been converted to a multi-gym); a 20 × 9m swimming pool; a solarium; a relatively small bar and cafeteria area; an external, floodlit training area, tennis and netball courts.

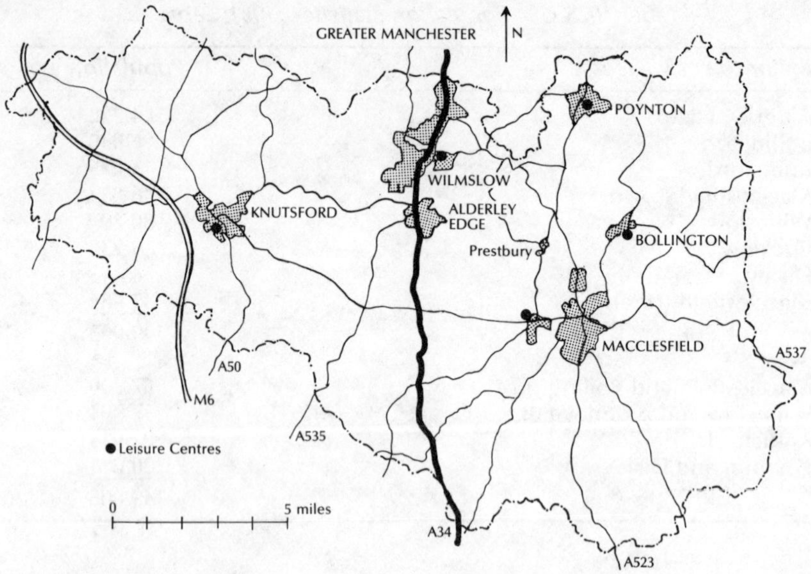

Figure 1 (CS.C) Sketch map of the borough of Macclesfield

The centre could also use a small gymnasium in the main school area which was large enough for one badminton court.

Wilmslow Centre

Wilmslow had a relatively new centre with a sports hall which could be converted very quickly into a 528-seat concert hall/theatre. Part of the funding for the centre had come from a charitable donation given on condition that the sports hall be made available for theatrical use for certain periods in the year. The sports hall was large enough for four badminton courts. The centre also had a 25 × 12m swimming pool with an adjoining learner pool of 9 × 6m; four squash courts; a large and impressive bar area with a catering facility offering hot meals and snacks; a large multi-purpose area named the Rectory Suite (with its own bar) which could be subdivided into smaller units by moving floor-to-ceiling room dividers, used for marshall arts, keep fit and social functions; four squash courts and a solarium.

Macclesfield Centre

Macclesfield leisure centre represented the largest and newest development. The main hall (36 × 32m) was large enough for eight badminton courts and was also used as a 1000 seat hall. The hall contained a climbing wall suitable for mountaineering training. The other facilities included six squash courts; a multi-gym; the Priory Suite, which like Wilmslow's Rectory Suite, could be subdivided into smaller units; a cafeteria and bar.

In 1985 the Macclesfield centre was undergoing a major expansion. A large pool area with three pools, including one with electronic timing, and an ozone treatment system was being built along with a projectile range (for rifle shooting, for example). Until the new pools opened in 1986, swimmers could continue to use the older pool at Macclesfield baths towards the centre of the town.

All centres had their own offstreet parking, only Wilmslow made a charge for parking which was refundable against payment for a centre activity. The charge was made because the centre was adjacent to the main road into the centre of the town and near enough to that busy centre to be attractive to park for a shopping trip.

The two largest centres were impressive modern buildings. Even the two joint-use centres were well appointed, although the general appearance of the Knutsford centre had received some criticism. The new manager there was undertaking some refurbishment to 'smarten the place up'.

Financial position

Table 2 (CS.C) contains a simplified statement of revenue and expenditure for each centre in 1984/85 based upon year-end estimates of expenditure by budget areas.

Each centre showed a deficit on operational expenditure (Knutsford 33 per cent, Poynton 15 per cent, Macclesfield 39 per cent and Wilmslow 20 per cent). The deficit levels compared quite favourably with those from other local authority areas, however, the elected council members were concerned about the overall level of deficit and that it was growing, particularly as the new Macclesfield pool complex would add substantially to expenditure once it opened.

A review of the borough's financial performance in managing its leisure centres by (CIPFA) Chartered Institute of Public Finance Accountants, a national body which oversaw local authority expenditure, had made a number of recommendations including some which could be labelled as 'marketing'. The overall view from CIPFA, which was accepted by council members and officials alike, was that better marketing of the centres could reduce the overall deficits.

The objectives of the centres

Early discussions on the marketing of Macclesfield leisure centres between the centre managers and the borough's Director of Leisure Services centred around the issue of what exactly should be achieved through better marketing.

The managers took the view that social as well as financial objectives were important. For example, special sessions were often held for the unemployed or the retired at uneconomic rates, or even at no charge. A concert at Macclesfield by the prestigious Hallé orchestra (based in nearby Manchester) had produced a deficit which could be justified because of the cultural benefit to the community. Council members were also concerned to ensure that leisure centres were used to the benefit of the whole community. They sometimes lobbied managers for concessions to groups who might not be able to afford a leisure centre charge.

Table 2(CS.C) *Revenue and expenditure for Macclesfield leisure centres 1984/85*

Revenue & Expenditure	*Knutsford*	*Poynton*	*Wilmslow*	*Macclesfield*
Expenditure:				
Employees' salaries, wages and overheards	122 450	88 745	110 070	92 305
Other employee expenses	21 685	–	–	–
Repairs & maintenance	12 255	7 900	2 715	6 725
Improvements	–	4 500	1 500	5 100
Fuel/light/water/cleaning	24 595	22 855	55 140	23 625
Furniture and fittings	370	2 545	255	270
Rent and rental	11 380	16 855	33 205	26 245
Equipment costs:				
Purchase (new)	–	–	–	6 650
Rental	1 760	1 500	–	–
Repairs & Maintenance	4 355	5 040	3 885	3 740
Provisions (food, etc.)	16 840	23 740	17 680	2 300
Clothing and uniforms	635	435	690	425
Laundry	65	120	–	65
Other hired and contracted services	4 700	12 700	7 000	13 800
Car allowances	1 000	750	400	690
Advertising, printing and stationery	4 135	3 910	3 760	6 730
Travel and subsistence	75	40	100	180
Insurances	1 900	1 465	3 335	3 015
Special events	–	–	–	2 000
Membership scheme	–	–	–	1 000
Car parking	–	–	2 090	–
Grant rebate	–	–	–	1 000
Total expenditure	228 200	193 100	243 025	198 380
Income:				
Sales	27 200	37 395	31 370	2 600
Fees and charges	76 055	94 115	157 390	105 005
Other local authorities	48 160	32 355	–	–
Membership scheme	–	–	–	3 605
Management agreement	–	–	–	10 000
Catering concession	–	–	3 300	–
Car parking	–	–	4 500	–
Total income	151 415	163 865	195 070	121 110
Net expenditure before recharges and debt charges	76 785	29 235	47 955	77 270

The managers were agreed that marketing their centres should mean attracting more people to use them and, by doing so, reduce the deficit. This contrasted, they felt, with the view of some council members that leisure centres should be run at least at break even, if not at a profit.

One leisure centre in southern England, the Magnet Centre at Maidenhead, was reputed to be running at break even, before interest charges. This seemed to be being achieved by operating with comparatively low staff levels, by allowing a high percentage of block bookings by clubs and societies, and by encouraging outside individuals to organise events which they, rather than the centre, were responsible for financially. The centre was also marketed more aggressively, the choice of the new name Magnet being one of the innovations.

The financial picture of the Macclesfield leisure centres revealed in Table 2 (CS.C) shows that wages and salaries accounted for the highest single item of expenditure. Swimming pools were held to be the highest absorbers of labour cost, qualified attendants were always present as a safety precaution. Yet swimming was one of the cheapest activities at a centre. This was in part due to tradition, pools, as explained earlier, were one of the earliest initiatives by local authorities into sports and leisure and the cost of using them was kept low to encourage their use.

The financial deficit could conceivably be reduced by cutting costs and/or by raising charges, or changing the mix of sports activities. They could be reduced by encouraging greater use by better marketing.

Social and financial objectives were not therefore necessarily incompatible, although greater emphasis on the latter would almost certainly reduce the potential to meet the former.

The one snag with using social objectives lay in quantifying them. The total number of users each year was suggested as one measure, but this did not take into account the special needs of groups such as the unemployed. The cultural value of the Hallé concert was impossible to quantify although it was clearly far less viable financially than other music activities run at Macclesfield such as pop concerts.

Financial management of the leisure centres was largely through budgeting. Each year estimates were made for the expenditures required for each budget area listed in Table 2 (CS.C). Leisure centre managers were given a prediction of the rate of inflation to guide them in setting charges for the coming year. An estimate was made for total revenue which was used to calculate the expected deficit. These estimates and budgets were eventually presented to elected council members for approval, along with all other budget areas in the borough, as part of the process for setting and approving a rate.

Leisure centre managers were accountable for meeting budgets although there were no obvious sanctions for failing to achieve targets or, for that matter, rewards for meeting or exceeding them.

Management control and reporting

In 1985 a new system of reporting was being introduced by the borough's Director of Leisure Services. Each centre was required to report on utilisation rates for their main facilities (sports hall, squash courts, solarium, meeting rooms) and on the number of people using each facility. The type of booking, casual, club, short course, special event or school use, was also recorded.

Table 3(CS.C) Usage by activity for Poynton leisure centre (% of total use)

Activity	*1982/83*	*1983/84*
Swimming	46.0	46.0
Squash	14.7	13.6
Badminton	14.3	14.6
Multi-gym	3.5	3.4
Five-a-side football	3.3	3.5
Child events	4.1	4.7
Keep fit	2.1	2.2
Others	12.0	12.0

In addition, revenue figures for over 50 categories of income were reported weekly. Thus revenue for adult swimmers was reported alongside bar and vending machine sales and so on, all totalled to show the total income for each centre during that week.

Utilisation levels had become a key issue in managing the leisure centres. Clearly if unbooked squash courts, for example, could be filled, then both revenue and the number of ratepayers using the facilities would increase simultaneously, meeting both types of objective that could be set for the centres.

There were plans in 1985 to computerise the analysis of the income figures from each centre making the identification of trends more of a practical proposition. Earlier the Director of Leisure Services had investigated the potential for taking data directly from the tills in each centre. Appropriate software packages and the necessary electronic tills existed but their cost was felt to be too high to justify their purchase.

Poynton leisure centre produced their own comprehensive report each year. The report analysed usage of the centre by sporting activity in the same way as that required in the new reporting system, with the addition that trends in activities taking place in the sports hall could be identified separately. In the new reporting system this had been simplified to report only the utilisation rate of the sports hall as a whole.

Sports halls could be used for badminton, basketball, five-a-side football, rollerdisco's, cricket practice and even indoor tennis. Clearly the income and throughput levels varied by the type and popularity of each sport. In practice, the main uses were badminton, five-a-side football and keep-fit classes, with the first predominating.

Table 3 (CS.C) shows usage by activity figures for Poynton leisure centre for 1982/83 and 1983/84. Table 4 (CS.C) shows the percentage of total income for a sample week by source. No one week could be said to be totally typical and this one was in summer, enhancing the swimming revenue considerably and possibly depressing the squash usage somewhat.

An examination of the statistics for each centre revealed a number of trends.

Utilisation rates were generally low on Saturdays, despite the introduction of off-peak rates. Saturdays were generally regarded as a family day and the sports-minded often took part in outdoor team activities.

Utilisation of the Rectory and Priory Suites at Wilmslow and Macclesfield respectively was generally low.

Table 4(CS.C) Income by activity for Poynton leisure centre: sample week (summer 1987)

Activity	*% of total revenue*
Swimming	33.7
Squash	10.6
Sports hall	13.0
Gymnasium	4.4
Outdoor	2.6
Multi-gym	3.4
Solarium	3.8
Bar	10.9
Cafe	4.1
Vending	7.0
Equipment	2.5
Others	4.1

Bookings in sports halls took some time to recover after they had been used (perhaps for some weeks) for special events. This was most notable at Wilmslow where the changes of use to a theatre were a condition of the original funding as mentioned earlier.

Usage of the two 'fixed' utilities, swimming and squash, had declined. Swimming baths and squash courts were not readily convertible to other uses.

Block bookings by clubs and societies formed a low proportion of total bookings. Bookings by commercial organisations were very low although a computer company based outside of the borough had hired one centre as part of a national sales conference programme.

Marketing the centres

The attitude of the leisure centre managers to the moves towards more promotion of leisure centres varied. The Macclesfield manager clearly had his hands full with the new extension which was behind schedule. The Knutsford manager had been appointed relatively recently and was under some pressure to reverse a downward trend in usage levels. The Poynton manager had always a keen interest in the statistics of operating a centre. The Wilmslow manager spent less proportionally on promoting his centre than the other managers.

Promotional budgets were very low and did not merit a separate budget category (see Table 2 (CS.C)). Expenditure was combined with printing and stationery costs. The sub-budgets for advertising were, in 1984/85:

Centre	*£*	*% of net expenditure*
Knutsford	345	0.7
Macclesfield	950	1.7
Poynton	505	2.5
Wilmslow	530	1.2

These figures compared with national figures between 2 and 5 per cent of *net* expenditure. The Macclesfield budgets were spent largely on press advertising in local newspapers and free sheets sold and distributed throughout the borough. Only small advertisements could be afforded and these were used mainly to list courses available at the beginning of each new season.

Special events generally had their own separate budgets for advertising. Examples of advertising are given in Figure 2 (CS.C).

Leaflets, paid for out of the printing budget, were available at each centre to promote specific sports or activities. Press coverage of local sports was good in both the traditional newspapers and in the free sheets delivered throughout the borough. Frequently a sports centre would be mentioned or featured in press articles about local sports events or teams. Posters in the entrance areas of each centre provided another low cost opportunity to promote, both to paying customers and to school children using centres during school times.

The leisure centre market-place

Statistics on sports participation were issued by the UK's Sports Council. These implied that, on average, each member of the population was involved some 21 times each year in indoor sport as a participant.

Participation levels varied with socio-economic group, region, and age. They were highest in upper socio-economic groups, in the south-east of England and amongst the young.

Seventy-five per cent of children (5–15) and 50 per cent of adults participated in sport regularly. Four million out of the 11.2 million adult sports participants participated only in indoor sports. Males dominated participation in the ratio 2:1. While the average participation rate was about once a week, some 10 per cent used a leisure centre every other day.

Calculations of the catchment area for leisure centres varied from claims that a seven-mile radius was an appropriate measure, to claims that it was impractical to define a catchment area. In Macclesfield's case the semi-rural nature of the area meant that the centres would be more likely to appeal to a closely-defined area. Table 5 (CS.C) shows the attendance figures for 1984/85 by each centre and the census population for the surrounding area.

The attendance figures for Macclesfield exclude those for Macclesfield baths but both Wilmslow and Macclesfield figures are enhanced by attendances at special events. Attendance levels as a percentage of those that might be expected from the national average figures implied the centres were attracting around 40 per cent of customers for indoor sports.

Table 5(CS.C) Catchment area populations and attendances (1984/85) by leisure centre

Centre	*Catchment area population*	*Attendances 1984/85*
Knutsford	13 700	107 342
Poynton	15 000	144 745
Wilmslow	30 200	306 489
Macclesfield	33 600	199 000

Figure 2 (CS.C) Examples of advertising

Table 6(CS.C) National participation rates and predictions (% adult participating at least once in four weeks)

Sport	*1973*	*1977*	*1980*	*1983*	*1987*
Badminton	1.0	2.1	2.4	2.5	2.8
Billiards & snooker	2.0	6.2	7.5	8.0	8.0
Bowls (indoor)	0.9	1.5	1.4	1.4	1.5
Darts	2.9	10.1	8.0	7.8	7.5
Self-defence	0.1	0.2	0.3	0.3	0.3
Squash & fives	0.8	2.1	2.8	3.0	3.3
Swimming (indoor)	3.7	6.3	8.5	14.3	16.2
Table tennis	0.9	2.7	2.4	2.4	2.3
Athletics (indoor)	0.7	–	0.6	0.7	0.8
All indoor sports	10.6	22.0	23.6	25.4	27.2
Children all sports	75.0	78.2	79.1	–	–
All adult (millions)	6.7	9.9	11.2	–	–
Children (millions)	7.4	7.5	6.7	(all sports including indoor)	

Source: Leisure consultants and government statistics.

The competition for customers included other leisure centres in adjoining boroughs, private sports centres and use by clubs of other halls, and similar accommodation, for indoor sports.

The percentage of household expenditure on sports services had been rising faster than inflation. People tended to spend twice as much on sports goods as they spent on services.

Participation rates varied by sport. The main source of such statistics was the General Household Survey, the most recent available in 1985 dating from 1980. A specialist consultancy, Leisure Consultants, provided estimates of more recent data and also predictions. Most data was for adults rather than for all sports participants.

Table 6(CS.C) presents data on the most popular sports.

Macclesfield leisure centre did not offer all indoor sports. The rapid growth in billiards and snooker was catered for mainly in private clubs. Some private squash clubs nationally were being closed down and converted to snooker centres. Statistics on indoor bowls included ten-pin bowling as well as the indoor equivalent of the more traditionally British game of bowls played in the open. Table tennis tended to be played in youth clubs and darts in pubs and bars.

Leisure Consultants believed that further growth in badminton was 'held back by lack of facilities'. The high-roofed leisure centre sports halls were ideal for badminton but had to compete with other sports hall activities for time and space. Badminton was also one sport where participation rates among women were high. Participation by women in all sports was predicted to rise as part of a general pattern of changing attitudes to the traditional female role.

Squash had exhibited one of the highest growth rates of all sports in the 1970s. However, utilisation rates of the borough's squash courts in the 1980s

Table 7(CS.C) % utilisation levels for squash and sports hall

Centre		*1982/83*	*1983/84*	*1984/85*
Knutsford	Squash	61	58	N/A
	Sports Hall	71	69	70
Poynton	Squash	56	56	54
	Sports Hall	79	75	81
Wilmslow	Squash	65	69	57
	Sports Hall	N/A	N/A	N/A
Macclesfield	Squash	53	55	56
	Sports Hall	75	72	71

Table 8(CS.C) Numbers of swimmers by leisure centre

Centre		*1982/83*	*1983/84*	*1984/85*
Knutsford	Adult	21 164	22 864	20 674
	Child	27 404	24 925	20 876
Poynton	Adult	18 176	20 000	18 519
	Child	25 153	22 914	20 117
Wilmslow	Adult	30 003	36 235	41 486
	Child	34 992	35 734	38 396

had been falling to the point where Poynton had withdrawn one court from use and converted it to a multi-gym. According to a Sports Research Association estimate, there were 9000 squash courts in the UK, that is, one court per 6700 people, compared to a Sports Council recommendation made in 1980 for one court per 13 000 in middle-class areas and one per 30 000 in working-class areas.

In 1985 Poynton, for example, had six squash courts, three in the leisure centre and three in a private centre. This implied one court per 2500 population.

Utilisation rates and prices charged had been researched by the Institute of Leisure and Amenity Management throughout the north-west revealing a similar pattern of declining utilisation rates.

Macclesfield's charges for squash fell in the middle of the range for the region.

Utilisation rates for the borough's squash courts and sports halls are shown in Table 7(CS.C). Levels of 75 per cent for squash had been attained in earlier years but clearly either participation rates would need to grow or capacity to reduce to see a return to these levels.

Participation in indoor swimming had grown and was predicted to continue to grow. However, participation levels for individual pools in the borough had fallen (Table 8(CS.C)) apart from Wilmslow (figures for Macclesfield baths are excluded).

Statistics on swimming revealed three trends. The first, for an overall decline in child swimming, was due to a decline in the birth rate. The second was for swimmers to switch to the more modern and spacious pools such as that at Wilmslow. The third trend was for a higher participation among adults as interest in health increased and as the percentage who had learnt to swim increased.

The opening of the new pools in the Macclesfield leisure centre was expected to produce a fall in utilisation at pools in the other three centres.

Charges for swimming and other sports did not vary significantly between centres and were neither cheap nor expensive by comparison with those made in adjoining boroughs. The charging methods varied slightly. Macclesfield had a membership scheme where, for an annual fee, members received free entry and other benefits. Non-members paid a 15p admission charge. The difference in charging methods did not seem to have affected usage levels one way or another.

Table 9(CS.C) details the charges for Wilmslow leisure centre as an example. The revenue per visit by a member of the public was fairly low at between one and two pounds a time. If leisure centres were regarded as specialist retailers (of sports services), this represented levels an order of magnitude lower than for any of the more successful high street retailers, for example.

Promotional expenditure would need to be either very low per resident or highly targeted to be cost effective. The methods employed would also have to be acceptable to the councillors who would need to approve any promotional plan.

Without first setting objectives for the centres it would be difficult to assess the success or otherwise of any promotion and to decide how to target that same promotion.

Table 9(CS.C) Wilmslow leisure centre scale of charges

Swimming	Adult	65p
	Junior	45p
	Mother & baby sessions	70p
	School rate	20p
Squash	Peak – 40 mins	£ 2.20
	Off-peak – 40 mins	£ 1.60
	Lunch-time – 30 mins	£ 1.60
	Junior rate	£ 1.00
	School rate	60p
Badminton	Peak – 1 hour	£ 2.40
	Off-peak – 1 hour	£ 1.70
	Junior rate – 1 hour	£ 1.00
Sports hall	Peak – 1 hour	£10.00
	Off-peak – 1 hour	£ 6.80
Table tennis	Peak – 1 hour	£ 1.00
	Off-peak – 1 hour	70p
	Junior rate – 1 hour	60p
	Ladies' morning	£ 1.00

	Aerobics – 3/4 hour	£ 1.25
	Aerobics – 1 hour	£ 1.50
	Yoga – 1.1/2 hour	70p
	Old Tyme Dancing – 2 hours	40p
Junior courses	Gymnastics £10 = 10 × 1 hour lessons	
	Badminton £10 = 10 × 1 hour lessons	
	Squash £10 = 8 × 1 hour lessons	
	Trampoline £15 = 10 × 1 1/2 hour lessons	
	Swimming £12.50 = 10 × 1/2 hour lessons	
Adult courses	Badminton £10 = 10 × 1 hour lessons	
	Squash £14 = 8 × 1 hour lessons	
	Swimming £15 = 10 × 3/4 hour lessons	
Rectory Suite	Full Area – Peak £20.00 per hour	
	Half Area – Peak £10.00 per hour	
	Full Area – Off-peak £10.00 per hour	
	Half Area – Off-peak £ 5.00 per hour	
	Special events/commercial, by negotiation	
Theatre hire	£225 per day	
	£950 full week	

CASE STUDY D

*Convenience Trading: the Rusts' Way**

The history and ownership

The man behind the success story.

John Emeny, managing director of the Swindon-based company, talked about his background.

> In 1958, after an apprenticeship with a small private group and further training with Sainsburys and Fine Fare, I joined a small company called Murdoch Norton, and by the time we had six stores I was managing director. In the early 1960s we came together with the Wavy Line wholesaler Kinloch and became their retail division. Trading successfully under the group banner I continued as managing director and was responsible for building a group of 60 shops. The Norfolk-based chain of Rusts stores was absorbed into the group. The Kinloch group was acquired by Booker in 1976 and I was transferred to Budgen as managing director. I didn't stay long. I was persuaded by a distinguished VG retailer, Tom Hendrick, to strike out on my own and bought two of his shops in the Swindon area. Three years later when Booker were dismantling their small shop division which was then trading under the Rusts banner, I negotiated the purchase of 21 shops and the right to trade under the Rusts name.

In 1988 10 per cent of the shops in Rusts were held by Emeny's working partner, Derek Marchant, who is assistant managing director and responsible for the day-to-day operation of the stores. Ten per cent was also owned by 78-year-old Douglas Scarfe, who used to be chairman of Kinloch. Emeny and his wife Charlotte owned the remaining 80 per cent split equally.

* This case study is based substantially on material prepared by John Emeny of Rusts (to whom we are most grateful for allowing us to use copyright material) and illustrates the development of convenience retailing in the independent sector.

This case study looks in detail at the development of the business between 1986 and 1988. It demonstrates how a small retailer can exploit 'convenience' trading as a strategy for business survival and growth.

Rusts in 1986

John Emeny was originally firmly opposed to the idea of convenience trading: as an independent grocer, he did not particularly want to open his shops late at night and on Sundays.

It also appeared to him that convenience operators were being unnecessarily opportunist, forcing other, more traditional retailers out of business.

His change of heart came when he realised his businesses was no longer growing: that he would have to sell off some shops to maintain his profit position.

He began to look at convenience stores afresh – for ideas and tips that might revitalise his shops:

> What impressed me was that operations like Sperrings and 7-Eleven created such an exciting environment in their stores. Apart from this, my wife and I went out one Sunday and noticed that the busiest shops were the neighbourhood stores with a strong food base, such as Eight Till Late.

These of course were not too far removed from the shops he already owned – 16 small grocery stores, all of them former Wavy Lines, which used the old Booker-owned name 'Rusts' on their fascias.

What finally convinced him he should act was when a shop he had sold became a highly successful Eight Till Late. Under Emeny's ownership it took £4000 a week as a traditional grocers but its new owners more than quadrupled this figure – to £18 000.

The switch to convenience trading

His first step was to ask for help from Booker, his wholesaler, with which he had already established a strong relationship. 'Booker helped me in the direction of convenience trading. In the early planning stages they gave me a great deal of assistance.'

A uniform image

It was Booker, too, which put him in touch with John Harris, who had joined Wiltshire marketing consultants SG Advertising & Marketing from Amalgamated Foods where he had been in charge of developing VG's Late Stop fascia.

Harris came up with a common design for new Rusts convenience stores. The colour scheme inside was red, green and yellow while shop windows feature diagonal 'decals' indicating opening hours and what they sell.

They were deliberately designed to feel spacious. This was encouraged by low gondolas which allowed shoppers to survey the entire store and head for what they wanted immediately.

Hanging from ceilings Emeny put up boards emphasising the benefits of convenience trading: 'Welcome to easy shopping', 'Everything for modern eating', 'What you want at a time when you need it', and 'Open 8a.m.–9p.m.

every day'. The signs cost £1000 and Emeny bought enough of them to furnish all 16 stores.

He employed Elliots of Portsmouth to do the graphics and posters, and a local artist to do the handwriting for the small price labels on the shelves.

The success of the new concept was immediate and Emeny announced plans to convert three more of his stores by the end of May, and two more by the end of August.

While Emeny realised that multiples were taking business from small independents, he was convinced there was still room for small stores to function alongside the 'big boys' complementing supermarkets, rather than trying to compete with them.

'In between their weekly or fortnightly visits to supermarkets, customers pop into their neighbourhood shops to top up. My stores are offering a different service, a convenient service.'

The transformation of the stores did not meet without some resentment however. Some smaller operators near his shop in Tilehurst in Berkshire for example complained that he was taking away their business, with the extended opening hours and wider product range. Emeny was quick to point out to them that he was simply responding to changing consumer demand as any business should be striving to do.

Prices were kept consistent throughout all his stores, and were competitive on the known-value items (KVIs) with Heinz Baked Beans selling at 24p and Andrex at 59p.

'Any retailer should be able to make a 17 per cent margin, and then add to it on other convenience items,' Emeny says.

The average margin in the convenience stores was now 20 per cent – 2 per cent better than the figure achieved when they were traditional grocers.

Focus on one store: Covingham

Covingham, a suburb of Swindon in Wiltshire, was where Emeny had his office – above the site of the first Rusts convenience store which opened on 1 December 1985.

The 2400 sq. ft store was on a parade of shops which included a video specialist, a chemist which closed at 5.30 p.m., a confectioners, tobacconist and newsagent, launderette, betting shop and a pub. The car parking facilities were also good.

Emeny felt the shop was too big for an 'ideal' convenience store, ideal size being around 1500 sq. ft, but persisted with the convenience face-lift.

In less than a year a 30 000 sq. ft Sainsbury was scheduled to open nearby. However, Emeny was unperturbed. He stated that by the time Sainsbury arrived, his store would be turning over £24 000. His confidence in convenience trading appeared to be justified. In one year store sales increased from £12 500 to £18 938.

Covingham, which employed 24 people, including ten part-timers, stocked 5000 lines. Emeny rationalised the ranges carried by all his stores when he converted them to convenience to make it possible to take lines out and still sell more because of the additional store traffic.

The size of the Covingham store allowed for a wider range of goods than in others. This included a good range of non-food items which were dotted around the store hanging from wires protruding from the shelves.

Emeny felt that wool, on which he took about £50 to £60 a week, and haberdashery were important to the neighbourhood lifestyle. He also sold books, supplied by Bookwise of Surrey, for the same price as W. H. Smith, and other non-foods such as bulbs and batteries. An 8-foot run of health and beauty products contributed well, especially when the chemist was closed. Cassettes and records, supplied by Oasis Merchandising Services, added to the rounded convenience inventory. They were all in the £5 to £6 price range and the latest releases.

To draw people in, a 12-foot run of bread and cakes was sited at the back of the store: a large Sunblest loaf sold at 45 p. An instore bakery was planned for later in the year.

But it was confectionery which has been perhaps the most successful new source of revenue since the conversion. Sold from several parts of the store, considerable space was given to bagged lines supplied by Sweetmate in Uxbridge. They put recognised brands such as Liquorice Allsorts and Fox's Glacier Mints into bags. Previously he only sold confectionery at checkouts.

Soft drinks were placed next to toys to appeal to younger customers while, for older shoppers, two new bottle coolers were filled with beers, wines and soft drinks.

As in all the shops, the check-out area was raised, allowing staff to see over the whole shop, as well as giving them a psychological advantage should any customers cause trouble.

With security in mind, Emeny decided against fast food. Even a coffee machine in the entrance to the Covingham store by the community notice board seemed to encourage loitering. The 'convenience' philosophy was imposed on all aspects of the store from product range selection to pricing and, very importantly, merchandising.

Focus on Tilehurst

The second Rusts conversion, the Tilehurst store, was in what Emeny describes as a secondary position. The area was predominantly middle class, but there was an Asda and a Sava Centre close by.

When Emeny bought the shop in 1984 it was trading as a Super VG doing £5500 a week. By April 1986, this figure had gone up to £10 942, and Emeny saw even more scope for development.

The shop was 2000 sq. ft and employed 17 people, including eight part-timers. On the parade there was also a greengrocer and a confectioners, tobacconist and newsagent. Despite this Emeny managed to take £800 from fruit and vegetables (before conversion this was £500) and £230 on video leasing – despite the CTN having a video section. Emeny felt video was more important to a convenient trader than news.

Just before Christmas an instore bakery was installed using Eurofours equipment. In the second week of April this took £700, which Emeny felt confident would increase with time.

When the bakery first started operating, leaflets were distributed to local householders.

The store design was similar to the others: at the end of the gondolas Emeny positions the traditional convenience lines, such as confectionery and snacks. To make old freezers fit in with the new decor the bottom panels were painted green.

The store had a licence and there was a 16-foot run of soft drinks and one bottle cooler. The shop also stocked a range of wholefoods supplied and merchandised by Country Foods of Aylesbury, a husband and wife team.

Emeny said the success of the Tilehurst shop proved that 'given a half decent site I can turn it around within a month and get good results'.

In both stores Emeny attributed much of success to the people. He considered store and company management to be the most vital area. The switch to 'convenience' trading could only be achieved with the full commitment of store staff.

He spent time and money recruiting the right people for the stores and rewarded them for good performance. He introduced an incentive scheme linked to the new convenience package with managers and staff awarded cash bonuses if they achieved certain targets.

'It is a case of getting them to understand that it is only by aiming for the excellence of Sainsbury in a much more human environment that we will be able to go forward.'

To help managers and staff operate efficiently Emeny planned to introduce a computerised ordering system. Because the Rusts range had been rationalised, managers operated tighter stock and ordering controls which computerisation would make easier.

In 1986 Emeny was confident about the future of Rusts – having discovered a convenience format that works. The next few years would see consolidation and then expansion.

Two years later Emeny's enthusiasm for 'convenience' trading had not dwindled.

By 1988, 13 of the 14 Rusts outlets had been revamped 'convenience' style. Despite the uniform facia, each outlet was tailored to the needs of customers in one particular outlet to be 'convenient' for them.

The business philosophy remained the same. As Merchant remarked 'people should be able to find easily the items they came into the store for'.

Emeny and Merchant were so confident that the 'Rusts Convenience' package would continue to work successfully that they considered the idea of setting up a franchise operation. The proposal would not only serve to expand the Rusts business but also help unaffiliated retailers struggling to compete in the face of multiple competition. Successful convenience trading in practice.

Notes and References

Chapter 1: The independent retailer

1. Bamfield, J. (1988) 'Competition and Change in British Retailing', *Nat West Bank Quarterly Review*, February.
2. Retail Research Report, Corporate Intelligence Group, 1988.
3. Burns, P. and Dewhurst, J. (1986) *Small Business in Europe* (London: Macmillan), Ch. 8.
4. Skidmore, K. (1988) *Towards a Taxonomy of Retailing*, Special Studies Project, Manchester Polytechnic.
5. Davies, B., Lecturer in Retail Marketing, Manchester Polytechnic.
6. Bolton Report (1971) Report of the Committee of Inquiry on Small Firms Cmnd 4811 (London: HMSO).
7. Swaffin-Smith, C. (1983) 'The Effect of Recent Employment Legislation concerned with Developing Individual Rights on Management Behaviour in Small Companies'. M. Phil thesis.
8. Ganguly, P. and Bannock, G. (1985) *UK Small Business Statistics and International Comparisons*. Small Business Research Trust (New York: Harper and Row).
9. Skidmore, op. cit.
10. Bolton Report, op. cit.
11. Kirby, D. and Dawson, J. (1979) *Small Scale Retailing in the UK* (Farnborough: Teakfield).
12. Jeffreys, J. B. (1954) *Retail Trading in Britain 1850–1950* (Cambridge: Cambridge University Press).
13. Mintel Survey Retail Concentration published August 1988.
14. Kirby, D. (1986) 'The Smaller Retailer' in Curran J. Stanworth, J. and Watkins D. *The Survival of the Small Firm 1 – The Economics of Survival and Entrepreneurship* (Aldershot: Gower) .
15. Verdict Market Research.
16. Lord, A. (1988) Senior Manager Business Development: Small Business Sector, Nat West Bank in *British Independent Grocers Association Yearbook*.
17. Atkinson, R. (1984) Support that serves only to Distort, *Guardian*, 2nd March.
18. Department of Employment, Small Firms and Tourism Division Ltd, Ebury Bridge House, Ebury Bridge Road, London, SW1W 8QD (Tel. 01–730 5874).

Chapter 2: Strengths and weaknesses of the smaller retailer

1. 'Independent Grocer Success Story', *The Grocer*, 2 April 1988.
2. Kirby, D. (1986), 'The Small Retailer' in Curran, J., in Stanworth, J. and Watkins, D. *The Survival of the Small Firm 1 – The Economics of Survival and Entrepreneurship* (Aldershot: Gower), p. 169.
3. Economic Intelligence Unit (1987) 'Convenience Stores Report' in *Retail Business*, 357 November.
4. British Franchise Association Newsletter (1988) Vol. 15, Summer.
5. Barnfield, J. (1988) 'Competition and Change in British Retailing', *Nat West Bank Quarterly Review*, February.
6. Jenkins, R. (1984), 'Ethnic Minorities in Business: A Research Agenda', in Ward, R. and Jenkins, R. (eds) *Ethnic Communities in Business* (Cambridge: Cambridge University Press).
7. Rural Development Commission information pack, including material re-published from *Woman's Realm* 1988.
8. Dawson, J. (1983) 'Small firms in Retailing: Terminal Illness or Just a Cold', Institute for Retail Studies Working Paper 8303, Stirling University.
9. Stoy Howard, *A Study to Determine the Reasons for Failure of Small Business in the UK* published by Stoy Howard Baker Street London.
10. Hurran, T. 'Marketing Strategy for the Independent', in the British Independent Grocers Association Year Book 1988/9.
11. Curran, J. (1986) *Bolton 15 years on: A Review and Analysis of Small Business Research in Britain 1971–1986*, Small Business Research Trust London.
12. Ibid.
13. Curran, op. cit.

Chapter 3: Retail strategy for the smaller business

1. See, for example, Jeffreys, J. B. (1954) *Retail Trading in Britain 1850–1950* (Cambridge: Cambridge University Press).
2. Ibid.
3. Davies, G. and Brooks, J. (1989) *Positioning Strategy in Retailing* (London: Paul Chapman).
4. See, for example, Porter, M. E. (1980) *Competitive Strategy* (London: Collier Macmillan).
5. Marshall, D. W. and Warren, R. M. (1987) 'Does the Independent Butcher Have a Unique Selling Point?', *Food Marketing*, vol. 3, no. 1, p. 107.
6. Ornstien, L. (1976) *The Retailers* (Associated Business Programmes Ltd) p. 173.
7. Sieff, I. (1970) *Memoirs* (Weidenfeld & Nicolson) chapter 8.
8. Kay, W. (1985) *Tycoons* (London: Piatkus) p. 10.
9. Senker, J. M. (1987) 'Technological Cooperation between Manufacturers and Retailers to Meet Market Demand', *Food Marketing*, vol. 2, no. 3, p. 88.
10. Anon. (1988) 'Over 10% of N & P grocery sales from Happy Shopper', *The Grocer*, 16 July, p. 30.
11. Lindquist, J. D. (1974/75) 'Meaning of Image', *Journal of Retailing*, vol. 50 (winter) p. 29.
12. Davies and Brooks, op. cit.

Chapter 4: Location decisions

1. See, for example, Davidson, W. R., Sweeney, D. J. and Stampfl, R. W. (1988) *Retailing Management*, 6th edn (New York: John Wiley) p. 255.
2. See the Open University/Training Commission video in the Small Business series 'Retailing'.
3. Consumers Association (1988) *Which Tax Saving Guide*, p. 65.
4. Campbell, J. (1984) 'The Late Late Supershop', *Retail Marketing Workshop* (Manchester Polytechnic).

Chapter 5: Store design and layout

1. See, for example, Rogers, D. S. and Grassi, M. M. T. (1988) *Retailing New Perspectives* (New York: Dryden Press) p. 453.
2. Mason, S. (1987) 'Out in Front', *Good Food Retailing*, June, p. 34.
3. Fiber, A. (1972) *The Complete Guide to Retail Management* (Harmondsworth, Middx.: Pelican) p. 96.
4. Omura, G. S. (1982) 'Strategic Design of Store Interiors', *Academy of Marketing Science, Monograph Services*, vol. 2, no. 1.
5. Murray, I. (1988) 'Dunns', *Intercity*, June, p. 22.
6. Open University/Training Commission, Small Business Series Retail Module.
7. Ibid.

Chapter 6: Merchandising

1. Davies, K., Gilligan, C. and Sutton, C. (1985) 'Structural Change in Grocery Retailing: The Implications for Competition', *Int. J. of Physical Distribution & Materials Management*, vol. 15 (summer) p. 3.
2. Higgins, K. (1983) 'In-Store Merchandising is Attracting More Marketing Dollars with Last Word in Sales', *Marketing News*, vol. 19 (August) p. 1.
3. Mason, S. (1987) 'Out in Front', *Good Food Retailing*, June, p. 34.
4. Cox, R. (1985) *Running Your Own Shop* (London: Kogan Page) p. 105.
5. Ibid.
6. Mason, op. cit.
7. See, for example, Lewison, D. M. and Delozier, M. W. (1982) *Retailing*, 2nd edn (New York: Merrill) p. 679.
8. Rogers, D. S. and Mercia, M. T. G. (1988) *Retailing, New Perspectives* (New York: Dryden Press) p. 444.
9. UK Government Statistics (see, for example, 'British Business').
10. Distributive Industry Training Board (DITB) (1982) *Mind Your Own Business* (London: DITB) p. 4.
11. UK Government Statistics (1986) *Family Expenditure Survey*.

Chapter 7: Pricing and promotion

1. Havenhand, G. (1970) *Nation of Shopkeepers* (London: Eyre and Spottiswoode) p. 47.
2. Cox, R. (1985) *Running Your Own Shop* (London: Kogan Page) p. 134.
3. Ibid.

4. Davies, G. and Brooks, J. (1989) *Positioning Strategy in Retailing* (London: Paul Chapman) chapter 13.
5. Fulup, C. (1986) 'Retailer Advertising and Retail Competition in the UK', *Advertising Association*.
6. Lowe, E. (1983) *Successful Retailing through Advertising* (Maidenhead, Berks: McGraw Hill).
7. Davies and Brooks, op. cit.
8. Anon. (1988) 'From Managing a Fine Fare to Running a Business', *The Grocer*, 19 March, p. 54.

Chapter 8: Purchasing and inventory control

A.
1. Information on Kwik Fit obtained from Company Policy Feature in *Macclesfield Express Advertiser*, 28 July 1988.
2. Davies, G. and Brooks, J. (1989) *Positioning Strategy in Retailing* (London: Paul Chapman).
3. Survey carried out by Harris International Marketing for six monthly shopping survey as reported in *The Grocer* magazine, 27 August 1988.

Other sources used but not directly referred to

B.

Purchase, M. (1987) *Talking Shop, A Handbook for the Small Retailer*, National Extension College, Cambridge.

Scott, B. (1982) *The Skills of Negotiating* (Aldershot: Gower).

Fuller, R. (1987), *Choosing, Buying and Running a Successful Retail Business* (Bushey: Phoenix).

Wood, F. and Townsley, J. (1983) *Managerial Accounting and Finance*, (Stockport: Polytech Publishers).

Chapter 9: The people dimension

1. Bolton Report (1971) *Small Firms: Report of the Committee of Inquiry on Small Firms*, Cmnd. 4811 (London: HMSO).
2. Sparks, L. (1987) 'Employment in Retailing: Trends and Issues' in Johnson, G. (ed.) *Business Strategy and Retailing* (New York: Wiley).
3. Ibid.
4. Sparks, op. cit.
5. Ward, R. (1985) 'New Shops in Old Areas: Changing Patterns of Inner City Retailing', Paper presented to the National Small Firms Policy and Research Conference, University of Ulster, November.
6. National Institute of Economic and Social Research (1986) *Young Peoples Employment in Retailing*.
7. Economic Intelligence Unit (1987) Retail Business No. 351.
8. Reported in *The Grocer* Independent Success Story series, 11 June 1988.
9. Newby, H. (1977) 'Paternalism and Capitalism', in Scase, R. (ed.) *Industrial Society Class Cleavage and Control* (London: Allen and Unwin).
10. Purchase, M. (1987) Talking Shop A Handbook for the Small Retailer, National Extension College, Cambridge.

11. *British Independent Grocers Association 1988/89 Yearbook* available from Federation House, 17 Farnborough Street, Farnborough.
12. *Employing People: The Acas Handbook for Small Firms* available from Advisory Conciliation and Arbitration Service, 11–12 St James Square, London SW14 4LA.

Chapter 10: Methods of control

1. Gloyne, P. (1988) 'Welcome to Midnight Express', *Company Newspaper* (summer) p. 1.
2. Knowles, A. (n.d.) *Electronic Revolution in Stores* (Ogilvy and Mather).
3. Anon. (1988) 'Shopping Around for an EPOS standard', *Computing*, 16 October, p. 4.
4. Knowles, op. cit.
5. Anon. (1988) 'Independent Success', *The Grocer*, 2 January, p. 29.

Chapter 11: Accounting for the smaller retailer

1. Dewhurst, J. and Burns, P. (1989) *Small Business: Planning Finance and Control* (London: Macmillan).

Chapter 12: The future of the smaller retailer

1. Barnfield, J. (1988) 'Competition and Change in British Retailing', *Nat West Bank Quarterly Review*, February.
2. Drawn from the summary in Curran, J. (1986) *Bolton 15 years on: A Review and Analysis of Small Business Research in Britain, 1971–86* (Small Business Research Trust).
3. Beer, G. I. of Nurdin and Peacock 'A Bright Future', British Independent Grocers Association Yearbook 1988/9.
4. Knowles, A. (n.d.) *Electronic Revolution in Stores* (Ogilvy and Mather).
5. Taken from the *British Franchise Association Handbook*, available from BFA Franchise Chambers 75a Bell Street, Henley on Thames, Oxon RG9 2BD.
6. *Food Retailing 1987* Institute of Grocery Distribution, Letchmoor Heath, Watford, Hertfordshire WD2 8DQ.
7. Gordon Simmons Research Ltd (1987) *Convenience Stores, The Fastest Growing Sector of British Retailing*, November.
8. Economist Intelligence Unit (1987) Convenience Stores Report 357.
9. Convenience Stores, op. cit. (note 7).

Index